"Someone has said that ... ... you hard and mean or drive you to Jesus. That's true, but there's more than that. Sometimes the dark will teach you about yourself, about God's love, and about amazing grace. There are those who have been there and teach the rest of us what they found so we can find it too. That's what Kendra Fletcher has done in a wonderful and refreshing way. As I read this book I cried, I laughed, and I sang 'The Hallelujah Chorus!' This is a book that just might change your life!"

Steve Brown, Key Life radio broadcaster; author of *Hidden Agendas* and *How to Talk So People Will Listen*

"Compelling, compassionate, convicting describe the story behind *Lost and Found*. Yet, as readers, we are lead to such a profound, transforming understanding of the infinite love and grace of God, our hearts are filled with relief as we are reminded that we do not have to earn his eternal love and companionship, but that his goodness and mercy follow us every step of our lives. Kendra's story brings life-giving beauty through each page."

Sally Clarkson, blogger; speaker; author

"In days where worldly prosperity gospel tries to convince us that suffering doesn't exist, and religious moral behaviorism says, 'God owes me,' Kendra Fletcher reveals the beauty and grace of God found in the midst of real pain in honest people. Her testimony of God using the catastrophes of life to draw her back to himself encourages us to see the hope that we are all longing for and can find in Jesus. This book is a page-turner of true hope and joy in a real world."

Jim Applegate, Pastor at Redeemer Church, Modesto, CA

"The message Kendra has to share is one that can only be described as 'desperately needed.' In a society laden with self-sufficiency and self-dependency, our souls are starving for the tenderness of being cared for by someone who *truly* loves us . . . not for what we can do for him, but because of his unrelenting grace. Experiencing heartbreak and trials beyond her wildest nightmares, Kendra shares how God reached down and helped her lose her religion and find the grace that was hers all along. He has that very same grace for each one of us. Kendra's story helps us see what it looks like so we can embrace it as well."

Durenda Wilson, Author of *The Unhurried Homeschooler*

"Too many believers aren't desperately needy for Jesus. They feel like they are good enough on their own. Through her tragic but beautiful story, Kendra describes how she powerfully encountered the God she thought she knew . . . a God who is close, gracious, and necessary for our every breath. *Lost and Found* is for anyone who desires a fresh encounter with God in their own story."

Barrett Johnson, Founder of INFO for Families; author of *The Talk(s)*

"Kendra's story of her journey to the cross drops keys of freedom into the hands of beautiful rowdy prisoners as she turns our eyes to the one and only Savior who sets the captives free. Read *Lost and Found* and share it with others, then watch as the prison doors swing open. A truly gospel-centered, Christ-exalting read."

Kimm Crandall, Author of *Christ in the Chaos* and *Beloved Mess*

"In his great kindness and love, the Lord frequently speaks to us with occurrences that are so much louder than words we're familiar with. He does this because he cherishes us and wants to free us from our false trusts: trusts in something other than his grace, trusts in the identity we've dressed ourselves in, trusts in our own abilities to self-righteously pull it off. Though this freedom is delightful we always militate against it, because we're terrified of losing what we think we can't live without. My friend Kendra Fletcher has been given that freedom and I'm so thankful; but the way that it came to her was as hard as anything I've ever read. Let me encourage you to dive deeply into Kendra's story and see the wonderful freedom that comes from loss and being found."

Elyse M. Fitzpatrick, Author of *Because He Loves Me*

LOST AND FOUND

LOSING RELIGION, FINDING GRACE

Kendra Fletcher

New
Growth
Press

www.newgrowthpress.com

New Growth Press, Greensboro, NC 27404
www.newgrowthpress.com

Cover Design: Faceout Books, faceoutstudio.com
Interior Design and Typesetting: Lisa Parnell, lparnell.com

ISBN 978-1-942572-63-3 (Print)
ISBN 978-1-942572-64-0 (eBook)

Library of Congress Cataloging-in-Publication Data
Names: Fletcher, Kendra, 1970- author.
Title: Lost and found : losing religion, finding grace / Kendra Fletcher.
Description: Greensboro, NC : New Growth Press, 2017. | Includes bibliographical references and index.
Identifiers: LCCN 2016038869 | ISBN 9781942572633 (pbk.)
Subjects: LCSH: Grace (Theology) | Suffering--Religious aspects--Christianity. | Fletcher, Kendra, 1970---Family.
Classification: LCC BT761.3 .F54 2017 | DDC 277.3/083092 [B] --dc23
LC record available at https://lccn.loc.gov/2016038869

Printed in the United States of America

24 23 22 21 20 19 18 17   1 2 3 4 5

To Fletch, who helped me in so many practical ways to finish this book, and who asked me repeatedly if my eyes were on Jesus as I wrote it. You point me to him more faithfully than anyone I know.

To Hayden, Nate, Jack, Abby, Caroline, Annesley, Christian, and Joe, who lived these stories and many more. May you always know that you are worthy because Jesus is worthy.

CONTENTS

CHAPTER 1

Perhaps the most surprising aspect of writing our own stories is coming face-to-face with what we fear in telling them. Honesty, even with ourselves, is hard fought, and yet the beauty of being freed from self-deception is really quite glorious!

—Kristen Kill

I found my baby in a coma. On a hot summer day in June 2008, while kids ran in the sprinklers, the air conditioner kicked on before 9 a.m. and the temperature pushed itself over the triple-digit line, I found my tiny baby boy hanging onto his tiny little life by a still tinier thread.

I was expecting this day to be like every other summer day: the kids in the pool, the laundry piled up with beach towels times ten of us. I washed, they dried their dripping bodies, I washed again. It's part of the ebb and flow in the domestic life of our bigger-than-average family. Our home sometimes feels like a freeway with teens in and out, families lingering on the back porch, door hinges squeaking as we go from kitchen to backyard with bowls of watermelon, glasses of ice water, salads, and burgers for the grill.

I'd fed most of the kids their breakfast that day, probably a bowl of cornflakes because no one wants a hot meal when the temperature is already heading for 100 degrees. I checked my watch. Nine hours seemed like an awfully long stretch of sleep for a seven-week-old, so I quickened my pace as I climbed the stairs to see if I could hear him. No baby noises—no crying, no little newborn squeaks, no sniffy breathing. I quietly pushed open my bedroom door to check on him. He was there in his miniature Moses basket, a thin white cotton blanket bunched up beside him. He was barely breathing. It was obvious that something was amiss. His skin was too cold for such a sticky June morning, his breaths were quick and shallow, and his eyes seemed to stare at nothing.

There was no way I could have prepared for the shock of that moment. It felt like I'd stepped onto the Tilt-a-Whirl, with the walls closing in, as if the bedroom was going to swallow me. I felt like I was walking through mud, in slow motion, down each step of the staircase, one at a time. Even after years of mothering seven other children, I desperately peered at my nine-year-old daughter with pleading eyes and asked her, "Do you think we should call 9-1-1?" I'm not sure why I thought she would possess more wisdom than I, but I wasn't thinking clearly. Who can think clearly in the midst of such an unexpected crisis?

I sputtered out the words to the calm, wise woman on the other end of the line. "My baby! He's not responding!" I said as I held his limp body in my arms. She was cool, collected, asking me questions and reassuring me that the paramedics were on their way. Three minutes, maybe, had gone by, and then four men, laden with medical equipment and prepared for the worst, entered my front door like a force. They instantly knew what I was struggling to come to terms with: this baby boy was very, very sick.

I stood in the entry hall, looking up at my thirteen-year-old son standing at the top of the stairs. I asked him to call his dad at work to inform him that we had called 9-1-1 for Joe. We packed tiny Joe into his car seat for the ride to the hospital and I stepped up high into the passenger seat of the ambulance as the driver took control. The paramedics were doing everything they could to keep Joe alive in the back, and the driver was politely asking me trivial questions to keep me calm. "Thirteen," I heard the older paramedic in the back yell forward. "His blood sugar is thirteen. Call the hospital; they'll want to know before we arrive."

"What's normal?" I asked the driver sitting next to me. "Sixty," was the quiet reply, and then nothing else. There wasn't anything else to say, really. He reached under the dash, turned on the siren and flashing lights, and we headed toward the emergency room at breakneck speed.

Inside that ambulance, we rode on in silence. Everyone was holding their breath and tiny Joe was too subdued for a seven-week-old riding in an unfamiliar vehicle with a screaming siren and three strange men hovering over him.

By the time the ambulance reached the city hospital twenty minutes from our home, my husband Fletch was there waiting for us. We did what we normally do in stressful circumstances, both of us snapping into business mode, he with a sharp humor that tends to put everyone at ease except us. We were dazed.

We soon found ourselves in the frenetic emergency room of our local hospital, where they were unequipped to help such a seriously ill newborn, where they ultimately could not do anything for him, where the charge nurse barked to everyone around her, "Get this baby transferred or we will lose him!"

Within an hour, we had called our family, sent out emails and text messages to those we hadn't been able to reach, and updated our blogs. By late that afternoon, Joe's story was bouncing around the Internet, and hundreds of people were praying for us. We began to get emails from strangers—concerned blog readers who had stories of hope to tell us or prayers to offer. At that point, of course, no one knew what was going on inside little Joe's body. There was no one to trust but God.

There had been fires raging on the coast of California that summer, and the smoke that settled into our agricultural valley meant that we could not rush Joe anywhere by helicopter. Instead, he was put into an acute-care ambulance, buckled into a gurney meant for an adult-sized body, and rushed seventy miles away to

Valley Children's Hospital. We were not allowed to be with him, so we followed behind. I'm not sure we said one word to each other the whole way there.

It was midnight by the time we arrived in the pediatric intensive care unit, answering probing questions from a gentle pediatric acute care physician who knew no more about Joe's status than we did. Working from the information and test results gleaned that morning at our local hospital, Dr. Montes couldn't see a clear diagnostic path. This kind and thoughtful South American physician puzzled with us, his head down and his hands wringing as he thought of what to ask next. No, we hadn't seen any signs of illness the night before. No, no one else at home is ill. Yes, he is a normal, healthy baby who has behaved just as our other seven normal, healthy babies had at seven weeks. "This just doesn't make sense." Moments of painful silence, then, "What about diarrhea?"

"Yes, he's had awful diapers today. I changed at least five in the ER," Fletch replied.

"That wasn't in the report they sent with him!" Dr. Montes seemed both worried and relieved.

Suddenly here was the diagnostic clue he was lacking, and Dr. Montes immediately stood to rush out of the room, a concentrated purpose in his step. "Sleep with your cell phones," he called back at us. "He may not make it through the night."

But he did. We awoke the next morning and looked at each other, amazed, and then we got dressed in the fastest race of our lives. We met Dr. Montes at the doorway of Joe's room in the pediatric intensive care unit (PICU) and, after we covered ourselves in blue gowns, booties, and surgical masks, Dr. Montes gently explained to us that Joe had been diagnosed with a deadly enterovirus.

No one knows how our baby Joe contracted the virus, but we know there was an outbreak of enterovirus-71 that summer in Taiwan. Taiwan! California is across the largest ocean in the world, and yet somehow, our tiny baby became infected with a deadly virus that rapidly wreaked havoc on his whole system. His body was in the throes of liver failure, kidney failure, heart damage, and brain damage.

One morning early on in our PICU stay, we arrived on the floor to discover the second hospitalist there, Dr. Kallas, hovering over Joe's bed and staring at his urine output bag, his brow furrowed and his pen tapping his chin. A tanned Greek man with a large gold chain around his neck, Dr. Kallas's deep brown eyes exuded care and concern for each of his little patients.

"It's stupid pee," he told us. "What we want to see is 'smart pee,' you know, because then we can be sure that the kidneys are doing their job. What Joe's kidneys are expending is stupid pee; they aren't doing their job of flushing out the bad stuff, and so what we see in the bag is nothing, really. Fluid. Stupid, not smart."

For days, we stood alert on "smart pee watch," imploring our friends and family to please pray for smart pee. It seemed so serious and not at all funny at the time, but now, of course, the thought of spending our days watching a urine bag and praying its contents would emerge from his bladder a darker color, reminds us of the grace of God in the small things during those intense days.

Then there were the wires. Hundreds of them attached to Joe's itty bitty head, like a baby Rastafarian with colorful dreadlocks and a skullcap. Neurologists, both in the hospital's monitoring room and around the world, could monitor Joe's brain activity to see what exactly was going on in there. He was having hundreds of seizures per hour, which of course raised the level of concern and drove home the extent of his brain damage. We were given a little clicker that was connected to his brain wave monitor and instructed to click it every time we saw any shaking or seizure-like movement in Joe. The neurologist keeping watch over that screen in another area of the hospital would then be able to draw an educated correlation between what we were seeing in our child and what they were observing on the screen.

He'd be a vegetable. Maybe. At the very least, he'd be completely blind because the dehydration and hydrocephalus he'd sustained had left a massive cavity in his occipital lobe, the part of the brain that controls sight and balance.

As we watched our baby losing his life, we began to lose our own. We could see, right in front of our eyes, on a screen, in a urine bag filled with stupid pee, how critically ill Joe was, but we did not yet understand how very lost we were, or our own desperate need to be found.

CHAPTER 2

It was now day five in the PICU. Joe was still struggling and certainly not out of the woods. One afternoon a young woman was rolled in on a gurney. She was distressingly thin, her large brown eyes bulging from their sockets unnaturally. Hooked up to lines, bags, and assorted medical paraphernalia, it was obvious that her journey had begun somewhere else. Her tiny, wasted frame belied her age; she was just a teenager, and she had been brought to the PICU to die.

Maneuvered that sunny afternoon into the room across from Joe, a few of her family members surrounded her and talked in hushed whispers. A young cousin giggled; a sister tacked a picture on the wall to cheer her up; a brother flopped down on the chair next to her bed. Was he scared? Angry? Emotions sit right at the surface in this place, yet it's difficult to understand the internal struggle taking place. Someone bursts into laughter at the worst possible moment; others break down sobbing even when the mood has been buoyant.

Soon after the young lady was made comfortable in her room across the hall, a steady stream of visitors began to appear at all hours. She was Hispanic, likely Mexican as so many from Mexico have made their way to California's Central Valley and settled here, working hard and becoming a vital part of the human mosaic of this valley, like the crops that form a lush and varied patchwork when seen with a bird's-eye view.

Pentecostal pastors arrived at her door, black leather Bibles in hand and tears already forming. I could hear the rhythmic mumbling of their fervent prayers and see them laying their hands on her, anointing her head with oil and pleading for mercy from the God they claimed as their Great Physician. They stayed for a long afternoon and she seemed comfortable in their presence.

There was the older Catholic priest who also obviously knew this girl. They weren't strangers, and she smiled with her thin lips and large eyes when he arrived. He, too, was a comfort to her as he swung the thurible containing incense near her head and prayed for her in Spanish. He sprinkled holy water onto her forehead and wiped it gently as it trickled down the sides of her face and little droplets splashed off the end of her nose. He held her hand as he sat by her bedside, praying, weeping, praying again. When he left, I could see his shoulders heave just as he turned the corner past her door. I knew he had succumbed to the emotion he had carefully restrained in her presence but was feeling so deeply.

And then a little levity: a tiny white dog was brought in to spend an hour with the girl, and she perked up enough to wrap her bony arms around its shaggy little neck and soak up all the puppy love she could absorb—a bright spot in an otherwise somber span of days. It was, after all, no secret to the girl that she was to spend her final moments in that room, never again to experience the gift and beauty that is nature, the world we take for granted when we are healthy and death seems to be in the far distant future.

For us in our little corner of the PICU, the workweek had begun and Fletch needed to be back in his office an hour and a half away, leaving me during the long days to keep a watchful eye over Joe as he continued to fight for his life. I spent my days in his PICU room, chatting with nurses, watching monitors, communicating with family and friends all over the world. During those lonely days, technology was a lifeline and a means of blessing as many people gifted us with encouraging emails and thoughtful little presents sent online.

And those many nurses who took the time to answer my feeble questions—they were angels in scrubs. Every night at 7 p.m. they gently "kicked me out" for an hour as their shift changed, using the time to communicate any new patient information to the nurse who was coming on for the night shift. That, too, was an unexpected gift to me. Without that hour-long break, I likely would never have left Joe's room, and I badly needed a gulp of fresh air and a change of scenery. My in-laws had graciously lent us their motor home, which we parked in the hospital lot, and it became a place of rest and refuge.

When the clock struck eight, I was walking across the parking lot from the motor home, in through the expansive glass doors and down the long hallway. The long-necked, smiling giraffe and Winnie the Pooh painted on the walls welcomed me back as my eyes looked past the photographs of local children and landscapes, a fire extinguisher, a water fountain. Turn left, pass through the PICU waiting room, and wait to be "buzzed in" to the unit once more. By this time, it had become a familiar walk.

On that particular evening, though, as I entered the waiting room, I wasn't prepared for what I found. It was packed from one end to the other with people who were crying, whispering, staring. Somber. Serious.

"Excuse me. *Perdoname*," I mumbled as I made my way through the crowd.

I reached the door and pushed the button to be buzzed through, rounding the bend toward Joe's room, but I had to edge my way along the nurses' station, because the normally empty hallway was crammed full with people. Immediately it registered with me why they were there, spilling out of that room and staring at me as if I had invaded their privacy: the dying girl was taking her last breaths, and they had come to rally around her.

Goose bumps prickled my skin. I quickened my pace, wanting to slip into Joe's room unseen. I slid the heavy glass door shut behind me. I mustered enough courage to ask the night nurse if the girl had died, but she wouldn't look at me. Head down, writing,

writing—she slowly shook her head as she walked away from her station beside our door.

Not a second later I heard a heaving, uncontrolled sob followed by agonizing moaning. I knew if I chose to lift my eyes to see what was outside our door, I would be choosing to take on the pain that now surrounded the girl we had come to feel such poignant sadness for during her brief days on our ward.

I looked anyway.

Two steps outside our door stood the girl's mother, doubled over, wailing and crying out in desperation over the loss of her beloved daughter.

I stood pinned to my spot by Joe's metal bed, watching in the shadows and listening to the hopeless sounds of her grief. I, too, began to sob. I had never spoken to that young girl or even to one of her many visitors, yet somehow my life had been intertwined with hers. Now her death was a part of my life too.

Have you ever had a pivotal moment, thought, or experience that sets in motion a revolution in your life? A moment in which the proverbial lightbulb flashes on and clarity seems to come where previously there was only darkness? A moment that illuminates corners you didn't even know were dark, and leaves you wondering how you ever saw things differently than you do now?

This was such a moment. I stood there listening to that mama wail in her grief, and I dissolved inside, looking eternity in the face, and thinking about how much time we had wasted on things that weren't of eternal significance. I thought, *What are we doing? What are we doing? We're arguing the minutiae of church practice—we're focused on religious stuff and our own behavior—when we should be giving people hope! We need to give people Jesus!* It was the beginning of a long turning point that was about to unfold for me and for Fletch, because up until that moment, our faith life had gone from gospel-loving to a "gospel amnesia" of sorts.

I'm not sure I can say when our spiritual lives began to move away from the centrality of the gospel. Certainly that was never our intent. But over time, little by little, we began to rely more on our own good Christian behavior for our standing with God instead of the finished work of Jesus. Does any real believer intend for that self-propelled wandering to occur? Of course not. But for us, each step we took toward relying on our own goodness, our choices, our particular brand of theology, our specific church, our methods, and just *us*, was a tiny but insidious movement away from relying on all that Christ had already done for us. The bottom line was that we really loved our religion a whole lot more than we loved our Savior. Somehow, watching that little girl die triggered that realization in me. I couldn't shake it. The Holy Spirit was turning my mind upside down, starting a renewal right there in that hospital room. For me it was my lightbulb moment, the first in a series of waves that grew into a tsunami that would wash away the narrow walls of our religious self-righteousness.

CHAPTER 3

How did we get to this point of a religious Christian life devoid of Jesus? How did the girl, raised in Fresno, California by first-generation believers fervent in their pursuit of Christ, and the boy, whose life was changed on a Santa Cruz mountainside during Young Life camp in high school, stray so far from the simple grace of the gospel and plunge headlong into religious self-righteousness?

I have known God since I was very, very young. As I look back over forty-five years, I cannot recall a time when I didn't want to serve him. Kneeling beside my childhood bed, my faithful mother would pray with me that Jesus would fill my every day. She would always thank God that he sent his Son to die for us; those words were woven into my life, day by day, year by year. I have always been a follower of Christ, and I know that somewhere along the line of godly parents, pastors, and mentors in my life, someone must have said, "Kendra, your identity is in Christ." But somewhere, I had lost my way. Somehow in my view of faith, the gospel—the good news of Christ's sacrificial death and resurrection on our behalf—was for the unsaved, accomplishing the work of salvation but not framing the life I lived as a Christian.

I'd been saved for so *long*. I didn't really give the gospel much thought after a certain time in my life. It didn't apply to *me* since I was already saved. The gospel was what got you "in," and I'd think, "Yeah, yeah, I know the gospel. Now just tell me what I need to *do*."

Fletch and I found ourselves jumping into the vast, deep waters of systematic theology, which is great. We all need to be encouraged to study the Scriptures, to know what we really believe, and to chew on the meat instead of remaining milk-fed and immature (Hebrews 5:12–14). Except that this should never be divorced from the gospel, never separated from our identity in Christ, never separated from Jesus. Fletch and I missed that part. We became *self*-righteous, not anchored by Jesus's righteousness. We were increasingly more concerned with the sin of others than with our own, blinded by our own "good" works and relying on our knowledge and choices to measure the depth of our spirituality. We sorely needed someone to knock us over the head and say, "Hey, news flash! Jesus is the measuring stick of your spirituality and guess what? He's perfect."

That's where we were spiritually when I found Joe so ill on that hot June morning. But I wouldn't have been able to tell you that then. It's beyond humbling to look back and see the grace God was dishing out for us in big, heaping bucketfuls, even though we held fast to the idols of our identity. There lay my tiny boy, swollen beyond recognition, hooked up to dozens of wires monitoring brain activity, putting out stupid pee, fighting for every single breath, and yet I didn't really understand the gravity of our circumstances. He was in the PICU for six days before I realized the severity of his illness. How could I not have seen it? It took the words "kidney failure," written in a late night iMessage by my best friend, to shake me out of my stupor. On night number six I lay in my bed in our borrowed motor home, weeping for my boy and his diminishing future. I know now that my lack of understanding was God's grace, a perfect bubble that protected me when the worst of Joe's suffering was happening. *Grace.*

The funny thing about the grace poured lavishly over me was that it came when I was smugly worshiping the idols of my own identity—wife, mother, Christian woman, homeschooler, blogger, among others. Yet God chose to smother us with his grace and peace that passes all understanding. He didn't wait for me to get it on my own; that never would have happened. No, he opened up the floodgates of his grace, poured out his mercy, and unleashed the power of the cross, *the gospel*, freshly blown like oxygen into my heart.

I didn't know how to identify myself with that grace, so I continued to build and serve my idols of identity apart from Jesus. The tricky thing is that some of my idols looked really, really good, particularly around those who valued them as we did. We moved along for years in those church circles without seeing our need to be found in Christ. Isn't that completely incongruous? We were so bent on serving Christ, on being good Christians, that we lost our way because *our* way was paved by our own works, not our relationship to and with Jesus Christ.

Take, for instance, our theological preferences. We had moored our boat firmly in certain theological waters, and we had developed quite an affinity for defining our faith by what we believed to be biblical. That doesn't sound too bad, does it? Except that we had no business defining our faith by what we believed. Our faith should have been defined by Jesus, and nothing else. It doesn't matter what we think, unless our thinking lines up with the gospel. Even then, it's the gospel that matters, *not what we think about the gospel.*

One noisy and festive Christmas Eve I watched with pleasure as my brothers and my parents opened their gifts from us: books by authors we approved of on topics like godly wifehood and, essentially, why the Reformed view of salvation is the only, biblical view. My brothers, both serving at that time as pastors in growing churches in California and Texas, were gracious about our gifts. But later the Texan brother wrote to us that he had read the book on Reformed theology and it had confirmed for him that he was, in fact, not a five-point Calvinist. We felt we had failed.

Failed! My brother has proven God's faithfulness over a lifetime. He has a solid marriage, he's taught his kids that Jesus is their only hope, he's traveled all over the world to take the gospel to people who haven't heard it before. He's watched men's lives changed in then-Communist Uzbekistan, where he and his wife played tennis as an exhibition sport so they could quietly share the gospel and why Jesus Christ is God and our salvation.

He's sat with students through snowy Quebec winters as they wrestled with God and came to breakthrough moments of freedom in Christ. This guy is a passionate follower of Jesus. I think he does, indeed, get it! And yet we felt we had "failed" in our mission to make another convert to *our* way of thinking.

In our little handcrafted theological bubble, surrounding ourselves only by Christians who thought and believed the finer theological points that we did, we slowly, incrementally crept away from the cross. We didn't notice how off-course, how lost we were at first. (How like our idols to deceive us!) But suddenly, when we stood over a tiny dying child, we saw that there was only one thing we wanted to define us. Only one thing matters: Jesus.

My husband Fletch is a thoughtful guy. He thinks, he discusses, he mulls over ideas and tosses them around to see how they stack up logically and biblically. He describes our theological beliefs at that time as "crystal clear but cold as ice." You could cut cleanly though our soteriology (our understanding of how we are saved) but once there, you'd find hearts as icy as a glacier. Cold to Christ. Indifferent to him, and feeling that a vibrant, joyful relationship with Jesus was for the theologically immature. As long as we were studying our theology and outlining our faith in so many points, we thought we were on higher spiritual ground. We would say, without a doubt, that we were saved by grace and that we could add nothing to our salvation, but we were living in a way that clearly looked down on those who did not make the same practical choices that we did. We labeled them as lesser spiritually, simply declaring, "They don't get it." We said, "Grace alone!" but we certainly didn't live it.

We sought "like-mindedness" with others in our church community, fellowshipping only with those who shared our view of the Bible, our theory of education—homeschooling was not only the best way, it was the only biblical way—and our views on gender, politics, the end times, and creationism. There wasn't room for dissent; those who held different beliefs and practices were tolerated but never truly accepted. They didn't "get it." It's all so appalling and shameful now, but it's where we were, and it all points to the real problem: our misplaced identity fueled by our pride.

What do you think happened when we didn't find like-mindedness on all of the lifestyle choices we had come to see as ultimately biblical and godly? These included Reformed theology, infant baptism, homeschooling, trusting God with family size (for some this meant "Quiverfull," or eschewing all forms of birth control; for us it did not, but it did mean we prayerfully considered each act of intimacy and each potential pregnancy), courtship instead of dating, and family-integrated worship (no Sunday school or youth group programs). We helped create our own church!

"You know what happens when you find the perfect church?" our pastor at the time questioned us. "You'll show up and it won't be perfect anymore." That wise Baptist preacher, who had seen six decades of religious behavior and lives freed by following Christ, was calling our bluff. He also had tried to warn us that, in his experience, homeschoolers didn't tend to "play well with others." I wish we had listened. Instead, we marched on, fervent in our good works, losing ourselves further in, well, *ourselves*.

*****

It had been a sunny day in late winter when we first had met as six families in our living room. This was going to be great! We were finally going to do church "right," finally going to have a place to worship and raise our kids that was safe and centered on the distinctives we felt would lead to our approval by God. Of course we didn't say that; we didn't come right out and say, "If we do *A*, *B*, *C*, and *D*, then God will know we are serious about our faith and we will gain his approval because we are doing church right!"

We didn't have to say it, because every decision we made was born out of the belief that we had figured things out theologically. Every church practice we chose pointed to how right we were. We deemed other churches shallow or downright heretical, because we were so deep.

Parenting decisions were calculated in direct proportion to our fear. Fear that our kids might be tainted by your kids. Fear that our kids might not choose the same church we had. Fear that our kids would date instead of choosing the approved "courtship" model. Fear that our kids would embarrass us and expose our weaknesses, those weaknesses we weren't supposed to have.

When we said we wanted "like-mindedness," we were once again showing where our idols of identity lay. If our identity had been in Christ and what he has already done for us, then we could have had true community that didn't need any other qualifiers. In fact, communities and churches built around anything other than the gospel are doomed to failure because focusing on anything other than Christ and what he has already done puts people into bondage. It doesn't free them to live in the fullness of the glory of God.

One bright autumn day, our newly formed church hosted a church history celebration, held on our large property and open to the community. These celebrations were always a lot of fun: costumes, petting zoos, live musicians, and once, a very crazy juggler who got lost on the way to the party and told off-color jokes. We thanked him with a quick payment and a goodbye, and then laughed quietly under our breath, vowing to check references next time.

A young family had joined our fellowship, eager to meet and worship with other homeschooling families. Immediately it was obvious that they didn't "fit" with the personalities already at play there. I don't really know how to explain why that happens, but it does, and people inevitably leave hurt, guarding their hearts just a little more the next time they venture into a church or group. I've watched this phenomenon my whole life, and have certainly experienced it myself more than once.

As we gathered that pleasant October morning to set up for the Reformation celebration that would welcome hundreds to our property, a tension materialized between a few of the families there. Suddenly, amidst the laughing and the party setup, the new family was getting into their car and speeding out of our driveway.

"What happened?"

Someone glanced at someone else. Two little girls—sisters—ran into the gathering circle and proclaimed, "Our daddy said we weren't allowed to play with her, so we told her we wouldn't play with her anymore."

My jaw dropped so far that I had to turn toward the house and collect myself. What were we doing? *This* was sheltering our kids from the evils of the world? Another homeschooling family who didn't do things *exactly* as we did, whose kids were a little more spirited, perhaps—*this* was our concern?

It didn't take too long before Fletch and I saw other behaviors and attitudes that troubled us, and I'm throwing ourselves under the bus with that statement too. I knew my spiritual snobbery was grotesque but I shoved it down into the darkest places of my heart to keep it from exposing me as the legalistic woman I had become. It was easier (and even therapeutic) to set myself up as the better one, the smarter one, the one who had her theology straight, the one who was parenting correctly, the one who was standing at the top of the mountain, reaching down to the less mature, pulling them up to where I was.

Before we were able to recognize those sinful attitudes in ourselves, we saw them in the people we were doing life with and, as other people's sin often does, it repelled us. Even though we didn't recognize those behaviors in ourselves initially, we began to "poke sticks" and challenge the lack of grace and the emphasis on performance in our church. As a result, we were eventually pushed out of the "inner circle" of families who had started that little fellowship in our living room. We began to understand what it felt like to be outside the approval of man.

Over the years, several other families had pointed out that the elder board was prideful and only a few families were really "in." We hadn't grasped that; in fact, we had mocked them for being immature and needy if they so badly wanted to be a part of us. It's intensely difficult for me to even admit that, but it's the raw truth and an accurate indication of where our identity was at the time. Our identity had been in being a part of the "right church," believing the "right" things, and behaving the "right" way. It certainly hadn't been in Jesus.

We knew other families who had been on the outside for years, for various reasons: the father was labeled "a typical uninvolved dad"; the kids had run as far as they could from the church once they had become adults; the parents weren't college-educated or homeschooling the right way or were using birth control or didn't believe in covenantal infant baptism. They were just never going to be "enough" under that system. That's the thing about self-righteousness. We have no objective standard by which to judge how well we're doing, so the only way we can feel better is to compare ourselves to each other. These families had been labeled "less than," allowing us self-righteous, prideful ones to feel "more than."

The tendency to compare ourselves to each other and to use that standard as our moral compass is easy to see in a godless world that has dismissed the truth of Scripture. It's far more difficult to recognize in our churches.

In *Mere Christianity*, C. S. Lewis said this about pride:

> "Now what you want to get clear is that Pride is essentially competitive—is competitive by its very nature—while the other vices are competitive only, so to speak, by accident. Pride gets no pleasure out of having something, only out of having more of it than the next man. We say that people are proud of being rich, or clever, or good-looking, but they are not. They are proud of being richer, or cleverer, or better-looking than others. If everyone else became equally rich, or clever, or good-looking there would be nothing to be proud about. It is the comparison that makes you proud: the pleasure of being above the rest."[1]

And there it is: pride and a need to feel better about ourselves. If I'm digging down through this story to find the root of our idolatry, those two sins are the Siamese twins that fed our idols and helped us lose our way in that decade of our lives.

---

[1] C. S. Lewis, *Mere Christianity* (New York: HarperOne, 2001), 122.

CHAPTER 4

*You see, it takes grace for you to realize how much
you still need grace.*

—Paul David Tripp

When I tell other Christians now about how we were living
during that period of our lives, many just flat out don't
believe me. I'll mention how daughters were not encouraged—
many not even allowed—to go to college because it was widely
held that the only biblical roles for them were to be a wife and
mother. Until that day arrived, they were to stay home and serve
their fathers. If you're assuming that that's a system rife with pit-
falls, you are correct. Increasingly, and at a sickeningly brisk pace,
we learn of young adult women trapped in homes where all man-
ner of abuse is hidden, where they are not allowed driver's licenses,
bank accounts, or cell phones. Those things are "worldly" and will
only lead to ungodly independence.

We know a young man who wanted to pursue a relationship with
a beautiful young woman who had been raised in this system, but
when he approached her father about starting a courtship with her, he
was told, "You don't want her. She's sullied and dirty. She's a whore."

We know of wives, even those in the public eye, who have no
voice when their husbands commit sexual sin. Instead they are told
that it was somehow their fault, because if they had only given him

better, more frequent sex, he wouldn't have gone to the website for those seeking affairs.

I'll talk about patriarchy, but those outside of this brand of the homeschool movement's bubble don't frame that word the way we did. When I say "patriarchy," I don't mean a broad social system or even a husband-led home. "Patriarchy" within the community with which we had aligned ourselves meant that the husband was to be served at all costs. His needs, desires, and decisions ruled (unfortunately, in some families, at the expense of everyone else). He held ultimate authority over wife, children, and property, and he should be the only one to vote for political decisions. I often handed my ballot to Fletch because I didn't want to make the "mistake" of canceling his vote if I voted differently than he did, even though he didn't care and in fact encouraged me to do my own thing. I was stuck in a mind-set that made me think he needed to make all the decisions. To his credit, he was trying to reconcile grace and a balanced marriage with that type of thinking. "Patriarchal" in our family came to mean husband-led, as in spiritually—as in laying down his life for his wife and children—because that's where Fletch landed on the issue. But that is not how it played out among many of our friends and fellow churchgoers. "Husband-led" often meant "husband-served."

We watched depressed wives sink deeper into depression, spouses with marriages in critical condition told that if they'd only read the Psalms more and try harder, everything would be all right. We knew of a porn addiction in a boy whose parents were in leadership. Once he discovered that we were on to him, he told his parents that we were a bad influence on him and he should stay away from our home. He'd learned by the time he was a teen how to manipulate and lie to maintain a facade of excellent spiritual behavior, but on the inside he was feeding his idols and trying to find his pleasure and validation in pornography. When the needs of the father are the only needs that matter, the door is left open to all kinds of destruction. And of course, when there is a standard of behavior to uphold, there can be no cracks in the exterior. No one finds freedom or redemption in a system that values behavior over the Holy Spirit's work in our hearts. But here we were, handing out checklists to fix sin issues. No wonder none of us felt we could truly, safely, be transparent.

But why would anyone want to be part of a system so devoid of the hope of the gospel? Why would we choose to dwell there? I guess we could point fingers at the parenting curriculum and books we read early on in our parenting, as they touted their way as the only, biblical way. But the truth is, those authors and speakers only fed our fear and pride, both deeply embedded in ourselves. Bottom line: We trusted our methods more than we trusted God. It's easier to follow a checklist and check off all the correct boxes than to listen to the gentle, faithful leading of the Holy Spirit. The truth is, we're all hope-shifters; we're all putting our hope in something from day to day, and mine was in my good religious behavior.

As we continued on a decade-long path of trying to do all the right things, we sank deeper into the despair of self-righteousness. We could not meet the standard—ours or anyone else's.

A few years ago I stayed in the home of a woman who was just beginning to co-lead national homeschool conventions with her husband. It was a brisk autumn morning, and we sat together with mugs of steaming coffee, legs curled beneath us, and the leaves falling gently outside her living room windows. We talked of our faith, of our families, of their purpose for the conventions they run, of our backgrounds and how we came to follow Jesus. I was telling her of that decade of our lives that had us so wrapped up in homeschooling and having babies and *behaving*. I told her stories of narrow beliefs and rigid dogma, of families in bondage to an ideology of homeschooling, dress-wearing, and a legalistic, outward view of modesty and courtship instead of dating (because dating is "worldly" and the system of courtship is believed to be the cure-all). I spoke of daughters not allowed to think about college, and sons forbidden to play on Sunday sports teams or watch the Super Bowl (on a Sunday) or work as a lifeguard because they'd be tempted by bathing suits all day long. She listened with wide eyes and the look I've seen many times before as I've told our story: disbelief.

A few months ago, I received a text from this friend. She and her husband had participated in a dozen or so conventions by now, and they had learned plenty about the modern Christian homeschool movement. To be fair, there are folks who homeschool who love to talk about Jesus and the gospel, who see homeschooling as an excellent tool for discipling families. I still run with that crowd. But there is an "old guard" too, one that says homeschooling is the only way, that wives must be silent in church, that children must obey even when they're adults, and that conformity to the accepted positions of theology, courtship, educational philosophy, politics, childrearing, and female modesty is next to godliness.

"Kendra, when you sat in my home and told me about your experiences within the homeschool community, a part of me surmised that you had to be exaggerating, or maybe just talking about your little fellowship out in California. Surely this couldn't be a majority mindset! I'd just never heard anything like that in Christendom. Well, friend, I couldn't have been more wrong."

She saw. It's there. Insidious. And as much as I'd like to say that it is just one little corner of the world of faith and religion, it is not. Just last month I was speaking at a large convention in Dallas. A fellow speaker told me that families in her workshops were complaining about those who were encouraging people to help their kids navigate the world. What we really ought to be doing, they countered, is to keep our teens from having access to cellphones or social media until they're twenty-one. I'm not making this up!

As I've listened to others who are learning to live out their faith in a way that never forgets Christ's work, they tell a tale much like ours. We all seem to know the gospel: that the sin of Adam opened the proverbial floodgates, or Pandora's box, if you will. That because of Adam's sin, we are all born into sin (Psalm 51:5), in need of reconciliation to God (2 Corinthians 5:18, 19), who is ultimately just, holy, and perfect (Romans 3:26; Psalm 89:14; Matthew 5:48). We can't even be in his presence because of our sin (Isaiah 59:2), but he has put into place a plan of redemption (Galatians 4:4–5). By the sacrifice of his Son, Jesus Christ (Romans 5:10), we are covered, clean, and made righteous before God (Genesis 15:6, Romans 3:21–2; 4:3, 5, 24; 10:4, Galatians 3:6, 11; Philippians 3:8–9; Hebrews 1:4). When God sees us, he sees his perfect Son (1 Corinthians 1:30), and all our sins are made as white as snow (Isaiah 1:18). We are then reconciled to God, through Jesus, not by anything we ourselves have done or will ever do.

That's the beautiful, grand story of Scripture: *creation, fall, redemption,* and *reconciliation.* It's not a one-time story that we tell non-believers or hand out in a tract and hope for the best. It's where we believers live, every single day. The gospel defines our lives and provides our identity with Christ.

But somehow Fletch and I felt it wasn't enough. We had to have Jesus plus our Reformed theology. Jesus plus our choice to homeschool our children. Jesus plus my decision to be a stay-at-home mom. Jesus plus giving our family size over to God. Jesus plus supporting missions, giving to our church, attending Bible studies. Again, we believed wholeheartedly that we are saved by grace alone, through faith alone, in Christ alone, but then we just continued on, wanting to do something. Surely Jesus hadn't paid it *all.* If we did all of the things we thought were so essential to our faith, surely he would love us more. It was simply turning our hope from Jesus to a panoply of everything but Jesus. We still are in danger of doing that every day!

Back in that intensive care unit, pacing the long hallways that form the perimeter of Valley Children's Hospital, I felt the weight of our circumstances pressing down on me. My shoulders ached. On the one hand, all of this was easy because there wasn't a thing we could do to help Joe. In that helplessness, I could acknowledge that God had everything under control, even if that meant Joe would die while we were there. On the other hand, my mind raced for appropriate responses. What sounds right? What sounds spiritual and biblical and *right*?

An old friend came to the hospital to visit Joe one afternoon, and by that time we had already felt the Holy Spirit stirring in our hearts. I remember her saying something about how well we were handling all this, and I replied that I just wanted more of Jesus and less of me. I could say the right things at the right time, but I had no idea how those words would come back to me in the months ahead. God was going to graciously and tenderly show me that more of him would mean tearing away the me that had built an identity on things other than the gospel.

The gospel makes it clear that we are accepted by God and secure in our identity with him because of what Jesus did. Because we are accepted and secure, we can begin to live in honest confession and repentance, reminding ourselves that our new identity is found in God through Jesus Christ *alone*. Our lives begin to change because we are camped squarely in the center of the gospel, and Jesus does the work of change, not us. The fruit of our salvation is of the Spirit, not of any choices we make. Will we make gospel-centered choices? If we are living in the gospel, then yes! But again, that's Christ's work, not mine. I had it twisted around to be exactly backwards: *First, there's a life change*, I thought, *then I would honestly confess, and then I would be accepted and secure*. But that's not the gospel!

Walking those long hospital hallways day after day, it was becoming clearer: Our acceptance by Christ and our security in Christ would lead us to honest confession to God and our fellow man, and then the Holy Spirit would change us! *That's* living in the gospel. But we weren't there yet. There was so much more that Jesus was going to reveal to us, and not only through our hardships with Joe. Sometimes, in the midst of an eighteen-month span that had us feeling like Abraham trudging up Mount Moriah,[2] knife in hand, I wondered what God's purpose was. Certainly, God was challenging where we had our identity placed, but that wasn't his goal. He was testing our faith, but that wasn't his goal, either. *Our freedom*—that was his goal.

---

[2] Genesis 22

CHAPTER 5

Joe wasn't our sweet, smiling boy anymore, but he did begin to recover day by day. He eventually had a PICC line inserted into his arm, threading up through his neck and down into his heart.

"Do you want to be present when we place his PICC line?" his nurse asked me one afternoon. I didn't even know what she was talking about. It's hard to describe how it felt to be in such a precarious position, with a voiceless, helpless child and relatively little medical knowledge to stand upon. I might as well have been dropped into the middle of Saigon without a translator.

Whatever that PICC line was supposed to do, it did. The greatest concern at that point, eight days into Joe's hospitalization, was that his kidneys would fail permanently, that he would have to be put on dialysis, and that this would be a part of his life from now on. That's quite a sentence for a baby less than two months old. Hooray for the PICC line! Hooray for a God who saw that whatever Joe's future might be, dialysis would not be an immediate part of it.

He began to improve, to have the wires removed from his head, and—yes!—smart pee. We all cheered for the presence of smart pee. A plush Curious George hung on the rails of Joe's crib, his wide mouth in that ever-present smile and his brown eyes sparkling as if he knew a secret, as if to say to us, "Don't worry. You've got a God in control of all of this chaos, who sees your boy, who knows his future, and who is smiling at the outcome."

We left the hospital eleven days later with a scrawny, recovering boy, a deep and endless gratitude for the people who had helped Joe there, and a giant question mark over his future. We'd spent many harrowing hours beside that tiny boy in a much-too-large hospital bed, praying, hoping, seeing that the only thing that could save him was the hand of God. We were exhausted emotionally and physically, but we had seen God move in Joe's life so mightily that we began to call him Mighty Joe.

*****

If June is hot here, August is hotter. Life at home had resumed, business as usual. Kids are so good for that. We adults can be stuck in our circumstances but kids push us to move on, to keep going, to enjoy what we have.

It had been several weeks since I'd been home to hear our screen door slam and wash all those towels every day. But now I was back to the daily routine. Sort of.

Two weeks after Mighty Joe was released from the PICU at Valley Children's Hospital, we took him back for a scheduled MRI. I had witnessed my son endure numerous difficult procedures during his stay in the PICU, and I knew this one was going to be just as wearisome. During his battle with the enterovirus, I had actually stepped out of his room several times because it was so difficult to watch them insert needles into that soft baby flesh, to hear him cry as they adjusted pain medication, to see that the fluids were puffing him up so much that we could barely recognize him. I thought his skin would pop.

We sat quietly in the imaging waiting room, privy to the many conversations around us. Over the blaring TV we could hear anxious parents speaking in Spanish, whispering in Tagalog, scolding in English. Little ones bounced around the room, exploring the brightly colored plastic toys and the well-used board books, as I sat holding my sweet baby in my arms, pretending I didn't have to be there.

"Joseph," the nurse called, not using his full name to comply with patient privacy laws. I found myself wishing she could have announced his last name too, because it would have meant that he wasn't a patient. That morning, I wished a lot of things could have been different.

I reached for my backpack and squeezed Joe tighter to me as I walked to the procedure room. I tried not to tremble at the thought of this little boy being slowly pushed through that large, cold, image machine.

"Go ahead and undress him," the nurse instructed. "Has he had anything to eat?" I replied that he hadn't; they'd told us I wasn't even to breastfeed him that morning. The technician strapped Mighty Joe to the table and then dismissed me. They would take good care of him.

One of the many beautiful acts of grace and mercy that God bestowed on us during Joe's hospitalization was the presence of my sister-in-law, whom I adore. Laura married my brother Jeff, whom I also adore, when I was still in high school. I remember thinking that this was about the best thing he could have chosen to do. Laura had been my summer camp counselor the year before they married. How great is that? My brother married my camp counselor!

Laura began a correspondence with me back when they were still dating, back when we all still wrote letters on paper with actual pens, back when she was an overworked nursing student at Biola University and I was an awkward, teenage theater geek trying to get through high school so I could get to college and on to the rest of my life.

Laura is a nurse at Valley Children's Hospital. She has worked there for many years, but selfishly I'd like to think that God put her there for Joe and me, for the days when we would find ourselves there again over the following years.

During all of those days we spent in the PICU, Laura was just down the hall and around the corner in the PACU, caring for children as they were coming out of surgery. Her large, compassionate, beautiful blue eyes were the first thing those babies would see. During her breaks, she would pop into Joe's room and love on him too. We sat in the lunchroom together when we could and I would pour my misery out upon her. Laura lovingly listened, and she prayed for my baby like a woman on a furious mission.

As I reluctantly walked out of the room where Joe's MRI was taking place and turned the corner to head down the hall, there was Laura walking toward me, smiling. She hugged me, rubbed my back a little, and helped to calm my nerves. She waited with me, and when she had to head back to the PACU, she said, "Text me when you're done, okay?" Sweet gift of a sister-in-law.

The MRI results, which didn't come to us for several weeks, revealed that the enterovirus had caused the formation of six cystic encephalomalacia (cavities, or holes) in Mighty Joe's brain: two in his frontal lobes, two in the median, and two in his occipital lobe, the part of the brain that controls sight and balance. We joked, "Well, he'll never be a gymnast!" but the sight issue was a definite concern and not so funny.

*****

And so the summer wore on, hot as usual and growing hotter into September. When most of the country begins to don a cardigan in the cool of the evening, we sweat. When New England posts fall foliage webcams, we're still practicing our cannonballs into the pool. Back-to-school clothes consist of shorts and T-shirts.

That September, Joe was three months old when we took him to the pediatric neurologist for the first time. He snuggled on my lap as we waited for the doctor to finish reviewing the results of the MRI he'd had weeks before. Doctor Ehrreich looked up at us and asked, "How much do you think he sees?"

"He sees everything," I replied, but I could tell that the doctor wasn't buying it. Dr. Ehrreich's eyes narrowed as he looked back down at the paperwork on his desk. Likely he thought we were hopeful parents living in some sort of denial, but I had raised seven other babies and was quite certain that Mighty Joe was seeing everything just as a normal three-month-old would.

The doctor approached Joe and pulled a colorful little animal out of his pocket, swinging it just within Joe's range of vision. Joe tracked it beautifully with his eyes, and Dr. Ehrreich pulled out another toy, again watching Joe intently. Finally he exclaimed, "Well, look at that! He really can see!"

Dr. Ehrreich finished his vision exam and then asked us about seizures: How many had Joe had since he had been discharged from the hospital? Had we witnessed any? Did we suspect any? The answer to each question was no, and he just shook his head. "Come here," he beckoned. "You've really got to see the MRI results I'm looking at."

Fletch is a dentist and is accustomed to viewing X-rays, but I've had virtually no experience reading MRI images. Still, no training was necessary to recognize the obvious deficiencies in Joe's brain; the abnormalities were astounding. I've watched enough episodes of *House, M. D.* to recognize that substantial empty areas of dark radiolucency—big gaps!—in an image of a brain were not normal.

"This is why I'm in neurology," the doctor was musing. "I can look at the perfectly normal brain of a child who is seizing 100 times a day and there seems to be no explanation. Your son's brain is so obviously compromised and he's not having any conspicuous seizures. And he sees!"

We left the doctor's office that day with instructions to let him know immediately if we saw any behavior in Joe that would give us cause for concern. We had a sense that God was going to continue a mighty work in our Mighty Joe, whose vision would remain a concern (how well was he actually seeing?), but he was most definitely not blind.

Joe is God's business, really. The brother above him was just five months old when I suspected I was pregnant. It was overwhelming to me; I had never had babies so close together. I remember taking a pregnancy test in the bathroom of our local grocery store, and when I got in my car, I called Fletch in tears and said, "I need you to be happy for me when I get home!" He met me on the front porch with open arms and said, "Kendra, this baby isn't anything God hasn't planned. He has a purpose in mind and he will provide for all our needs."

It was true. I had been pregnant eight times before I was pregnant with Joe, and each time I was dreadfully sick except for the baby I lost to miscarriage. When the weeks of that first trimester with Joe began to tick away and the morning sickness barely kicked in, I knew God was pouring out his mercy over my inordinately fatigued frame.

I remember hovering over Joe's bed in the PICU one night, all alone in that dark room, thinking, *God, Mighty Joe is your child. We didn't plan him, but you did. Use his life for your glory.* The knowledge that God had planned Joe from the very beginning made all we were going through far easier to endure.

I'd love to be able to tell you how strong, faithful, and good we were while we weathered this trial with Joe, but the truth is that we were very, very broken. Trust God? Barely, and only because God reminded us of his previous faithfulness in the midst of our exhausted resignation to the whirlwind that engulfed us. We were so bound up in our good works that it would take a severe act of godly mercy to pull the rug out from underneath our misguided, self-righteous smugness. Our misgivings, which should have blared a warning blast over the previous several years, were just starting to sound an alarm. Mighty Joe was just the beginning.

CHAPTER 6

The air was crisp, finally, after the long, joyful months of summer. I'm always sad to see the lazier days fly past, always hoping I can push summer later and later into the colder months. But I couldn't deny how warm the electric blanket was as I pushed the blankets off my legs or how cold the tiles felt when I put my feet down and stumbled to the bathroom. I wanted as little of my feet to touch those big, freezing tiles as possible, and I had to throw on a sweatshirt even before I splashed water on my face or squeezed the cinnamon toothpaste onto my brush.

I could smell the burn piles the farmers create with brush, wood, and harvest waste. It's an autumn smell, and it made me feel warm and cozy.

The autumn following Joe's illness came and went rather uneventfully. We were grateful to be home together and slowly we were getting back in the swing of our school and work routines. Homeschooling always demands a measure of faith and trust, and September is about the time I wonder what in the world I was thinking, taking on the responsibility for the education of all these kids.

We still felt somewhat shell-shocked, too, after spending so many intense hours and days focusing on the life of one tiny child. When you are forced to stop everything to nurture someone through a serious illness, the world outside those hospital walls ceases to exist. It's as if you're occupying an alternate universe.

Hours pass with your only thought and concern being blood pressure levels or white cell counts. Then, suddenly, you are thrust back into "real" life and there's no easy reentry. Yet we had to hit the ground running.

I still scrutinized Joe closely, and I didn't really want him away from me. Except for a few ugly bruises where the PICC and IV lines had been, he looked perfectly healthy, but my baby had been to hell and back and I wasn't about to let him cry it out.

By December I was feeling as though I could breathe again, and then, of course, Christmas arrived with all of its usual pomp and circumstance. All of the excitement and anxiety the enterovirus had brought with it that past summer was fading, and we were finally feeling that life could chug along as it always had.

It was the end of December, the air was cold, and the natives in my house were post-Christmas-craziness restless. Friends suggested that we take all our kids bowling, and it turned out to be a fun, even normal, morning. Kids were throwing bowling balls that were too heavy and rolling down the gutter at the speed of a reluctant turtle—lots of fun, lots of joy.

We headed into our driveway after the bowling adventure, planning a quiet afternoon of naps for little guys and perhaps a cup of hot cocoa or two. Our driveway provides the entrance to almost two acres of land, circling a large fountain in front of our home and continuing to the little home next door where my in-laws reside. Normally, I park as soon as I pull into the circle. Normally, our ample and trustworthy twelve-passenger van glides right into place. The doors are then opened, and kids spill out at lightning speed, heading for the front door.

This day, however, I was feeling more thoughtful than usual (normally I think only of parking the van where I normally do). I decided to pull all the way to the other side of the fountain so that Fletch could park his VW bus right behind the van. I was feeling pretty good about my good deed!

Normally, that would be a great idea. This day, however, our diminutive five-year-old opened the door and sat on the van's step, planning to jump out as soon as I stopped the van to park, but of course, I didn't stop or park.

The fountain is surrounded by a curb, and if you've ever driven a larger-than-typical vehicle, you understand from experience that running over curbs is a regular occurrence. As I veered the van to the right around the circle, around the fountain, I at once felt the back tire go over a bump. I heard the other children beginning to scream variations of "Mom! You're running over Annesley!" It was only a split second, with no time to process any thoughts other than *God. Oh God.*

Just months before, Christian recording artist Steven Curtis Chapman's precious daughter Maria Sue had been killed when her brother accidentally ran over her in their driveway.[3] Maria's story had been the topic of discussion and prayer at our dinner table, and we warned our teens who were learning to drive of the importance of looking out for the little people on our property. My stomach had been sick with distress and sorrow on behalf of that innocent brother who could not have known what that day would hold for his family.

And now, in that extremely brief moment when the reality of what I had done flooded my brain, when my fingers went numb and the horror began to sink in, all I could think of was the Chapmans' little girl and her suffering big brother.

Then I prayed, "Lord, prepare me for what I'm going to see." I shifted into park, flung open the driver-side door, and tore around to the back of the van, not knowing what I would find there.

These are the moments when our faith has to stand or be crushed. We either believe that God will deliver, that he will redeem, that he has already saved us—or we are crushed under the blows of idols we have substituted for God's power and provision.

I didn't do so well. In the moment, though, I did what I had to do. I reached the back of the van to see my towheaded, blue-eyed

<hr />

[3] Rennie Dyball, "Singer Steven Curtis Chapman's Daughter Dies in Tragic Accident," *People Magazine*, May 22, 2008. http://www.people.com/people/article/0,,20201819,00.html.

pixie of a daughter sitting up and crying. Sitting up, crying. There was no blood, no lifeless body, no tragic end that I was fully anticipating.

I urged her to stand up. "Stop crying, Honey. I can't help you if you're crying. Stand up. Can you walk?" She could. She stood up in the driveway and, after having been run over by nearly a ton of steel, she walked to the front door and halfway up the stairs, where I scooped her up in my arms and carried her to her bathtub, thinking I could at once calm her and call her daddy for direction and help.

Over the phone, Fletch asked me basic medical questions, helping me to determine whether this injury warranted a 9-1-1 call. She was not spitting up blood. There was no blood in her urine. There were no protruding bones and she was completely coherent (crying, but coherent). By the end of the phone call, she had calmed down, I had calmed down, and my husband recommended we take her to our close friend, a chiropractor with an office just ten minutes from our home, to have him examine and X-ray her right there in his office. The closest hospital doesn't have the greatest reputation, and our thinking was that he could see her most quickly. To us, that seemed like a wise and prudent plan.

We reached John's office and I carried Annesley in, cradled in my arms. The last hour had sapped her emotionally; her mother had just run over her. Her mother.

John felt for signs of breakage, and although he found nothing immediately alarming, he did recognize that she had probably fractured her pelvis. We agreed to bypass that closest hospital, opting instead to drive her the thirty minutes to the emergency room where the ambulance had taken Mighty Joe just six months earlier.

The hospital staff members were immediately concerned, of course, when they heard our story. "Why didn't you call 9-1-1?" and then the long explanation began. Someone there didn't like my answer, and the authorities were alerted. Suddenly my worst nightmare was becoming my second-worst nightmare.

At any given moment, as parents, we attempt to make the best and wisest call for the health and well-being of our children. Still, someone else may not agree with our choices, and here I was, facing suspicion and allegation. I had run over my child in my own driveway, and someone who was supposed to be giving us help was instead threatening my whole existence, questioning my competency in the job to which I had dedicated the last fifteen years of my life. My identity was in this job. They were questioning *my identity*.

A police officer approached me in the emergency room and began to ask questions. Once again I heard the accusation: "Why didn't you call 9-1-1?" By this time my ire was up—let's focus on helping my daughter already! I looked that man squarely in the eye and said, "Last summer I found my baby in a coma. That was a 9-1-1 call. I found Annesley sitting up crying, not bleeding, and completely alert. I monitored her behavior. I did what I thought was wisest in the moment."

The officer then turned his attention to Annesley, asking her questions to see if her story matched mine. When it did, he sat next to her and was kind and gentle.

Of course, the questioning didn't stop there, as it shouldn't have. When there is abuse, when a parent or caregiver does not have the child's best interest in mind, we are grateful that there are those who step in and find help for these kids. But when you know you would move heaven and earth for your babies and someone from such a watchdog agency steps in to question you, it is earth-shattering.

Or identity-displacing.

I wish that in the moment I could have let down my guard and realized that God had our back, entirely. I knew that in my head, but I didn't know it in my soul. I think we often live our Christian lives that way. We know in our heads that God always has a plan, that he always comes through with the best thing. We recite Jeremiah 29:11, "For I know the plans I have for you, declares the

LORD, plans for welfare and not for evil, to give you a future and a hope."

Take the story of Gideon and the Midianites. I have heard this story since childhood, and it's a stunning account of God's faithfulness and equipping, a true God's-got-my-back story.

Here's a refresher:

The LORD said to Gideon, "The people with you are too many for me to give the Midianites into their hand, lest Israel boast over me, saying, 'My own hand has saved me.' Now therefore proclaim in the ears of the people, saying, 'Whoever is fearful and trembling, let him return home and hurry away from Mount Gilead.'" Then 22,000 of the people returned, and 10,000 remained.

And the LORD said to Gideon, "The people are still too many. Take them down to the water, and I will test them for you there, and anyone of whom I say to you, 'This one shall go with you,' shall go with you, and anyone of whom I say to you, 'This one shall not go with you,' shall not go." So he brought the people down to the water. And the LORD said to Gideon, "Every one who laps the water with his tongue, as a dog laps, you shall set by himself. Likewise, every one who kneels down to drink." And the number of those who lapped, putting their hands to their mouths, was 300 men, but all the rest of the people knelt down to drink water. And the LORD said to Gideon, "With the 300 men who lapped I will save you and give the Midianites into your hand, and let all the others go every man to his home." So the people took provisions in their hands, and their trumpets. And he sent all the rest of Israel every man to his tent, but retained the 300 men. And the camp of Midian was below him in the valley.

That same night the LORD said to him, "Arise, go down against the camp, for I have given it into your hand. But if you are afraid to go down, go down to the camp with Purah your servant. And you shall hear what they say, and afterward your hands shall be strengthened to go down against the camp." Then he went down with Purah his servant to the outposts of the armed men who were in the camp. And the Midianites and the Amalekites and all the people of the East lay along the valley like locusts in abundance, and their camels were without number, as the sand that is on the seashore in abundance. When Gideon came, behold, a man was telling a dream to his comrade. And he said, "Behold, I dreamed a dream, and behold, a cake of barley bread tumbled into the camp of Midian and came to the tent and struck it so that it fell and turned it upside down, so that the tent lay flat." And his comrade answered, "This is no other than the sword of Gideon the son of Joash, a man of Israel; God has given into his hand Midian and all the camp."

As soon as Gideon heard the telling of the dream and its interpretation, he worshiped. And he returned to the camp of Israel and said, "Arise, for the Lord has given the host of Midian into your hand." And he divided the 300 men into three companies and put trumpets into the hands of all of them and empty jars, with torches inside the jars. And he said to them, "Look at me, and do likewise. When I come to the outskirts of the camp, do as I do. When I blow the trumpet, I and all who are with me, then blow the trumpets also on every side of all the camp and shout, 'For the Lord and for Gideon.'"

So Gideon and the hundred men who were with him came to the outskirts of the camp at the beginning of the middle watch, when they had just set the watch. And they blew the trumpets and smashed the jars that were in their hands. Then the three companies blew the trumpets and broke the jars. They held in their left hands the torches, and in their right hands the trumpets to blow. And they cried out, "A sword for the Lord and for Gideon!" Every man stood in his place around the camp, and all the army ran. They cried out and fled. When they blew the 300 trumpets, the Lord set every man's sword against his comrade and against all the army. And the army fled as far as Beth-shittah

toward Zererah, as far as the border of Abel-meholah,
by Tabbath. And the men of Israel were called out from
Naphtali and from Asher and from all Manasseh, and they
pursued after Midian.

Gideon sent messengers throughout all the hill country
of Ephraim, saying, "Come down against the Midianites and
capture the waters against them, as far as Beth-barah, and
also the Jordan." So all the men of Ephraim were called out,
and they captured the waters as far as Beth-barah, and also
the Jordan. And they captured the two princes of Midian,
Oreb and Zeeb. They killed Oreb at the rock of Oreb, and
Zeeb they killed at the winepress of Zeeb. Then they pursued
Midian, and they brought the heads of Oreb and Zeeb to
Gideon across the Jordan. (Judges 7:2–25)

Three hundred men. Three hundred Israelites up against an
army that was prepared to squash them even if they had numbered
in the tens of thousands. We, reading our Bibles and grasping the
numbers, realize what a marvelous act of God this was, but when
we face our own Midianite army, we look for help from all kinds of
other sources, not really understanding that when we do that, we
are shifting our hope from the One who saves to the many tools he
may provide for us along the way.

There I was, facing my Midianite army in the form of a social
worker, who was summoned because someone at the hospital was
concerned that I didn't drive my sweet girl straight to their doorstep.
What would I do? Would I truly, deeply trust the God who plans
such exceptional and wonderful escapes as an army stumbling in the
darkness, killing off their own men? Or would I shift my hope to
everything but him: social worker, doctors, nurses, police officer—
those who seemed to hold Annesley's future in their hands?

CHAPTER 7

Once again we were transferred to the children's hospital where Mighty Joe had spent so many days, but this time Fletch remained at home with the other children, mostly because the social worker assigned to meet with us at the hospital needed to visit our home that evening.

After an uneventful two-hour ambulance ride, Annesley and I sat together in the emergency room awaiting X-ray results, which confirmed our chiropractor's diagnosis: a fractured pelvis. We were admitted for the night, but not without first speaking with the social worker, who obviously wished to assume the best about our accident. Someone had told her that our baby had died last summer, and I just couldn't believe how the emergency room in our hometown had continued to get our story so wrong. It feels terrible to have one's integrity questioned; it feels just as bad to realize that they're not even getting the facts straight. It seemed to me that my Midianite army was growing in size.

Lying on a pull-out bed next to Annesley, I spent that night in a miserable, nervous, sleepless state. I was in the same sweater I'd thrown on to go bowling, without a toothbrush or soap to wash the makeup off my face. I texted Fletch, "What happened with the social worker?" His reply was a glowing report of a kind man who knew before he even left the emergency room that this was a moot case. He'd witnessed all the kids bounding toward their dad when he arrived home (would abused children lavish affection upon and be so excited to see a father who abused them?) and, after interviewing the kids, he said his report wouldn't even be filed. But I still didn't sleep well.

My little bubble had been burst. My identity as a good mother had been ripped out from under me. Someone had questioned my skill at mothering, and that criticism had shaken me so profoundly that I couldn't help but replay the incident over and over in my mind.

In the process, I missed the whole point! This story, our story, our future—it's all about Jesus and our identity in him. That's where our freedom is gained, because he has already bought and paid for my sin with his own sacrifice. Even if I had made the best choices concerning Annesley, Mighty Joe, or any of our other children, it was still about Jesus and never, never about me. I knew this, yet I didn't *know* this.

Doctors cannot put casts on fractured pelvises, so Annesley was released to spend six weeks off her feet and on the couch at home. Her rented red wheelchair was the tiniest we had ever seen, and by the second week of no walking, she had abandoned the chair for scooting herself along the floor.

Each day dragged for her; she was like a little girl lugging along sandbags heavy from a deluge of winter rain.

Lug, lug. "Whyyyyy can't I scooch along the kitchen floor?"

Lug. Lug. Lug. "Wheennnn do I get to walk again? How many days left?"

Asking a precocious five-year-old to be content on the couch while seven other children march on is a ridiculously tall order. Annesley lent her dramatic personality to every minute.

Overall, she did remarkably well, but there were moments of high histrionics. Friends stopped by with dinner and gifts, videos and Lite-Brites, activity books and crayons. Finally—finally!—six weeks were up and we returned to Valley Children's Hospital to visit the pediatric orthopedist who had reviewed her case on the night of the accident.

He seemed casual to me. I had my doubts about the severity of Annesley's injuries, so I queried, "How serious was this fracture?" He replied, "Well, let me put it this way: If these were prehistoric times and a boulder had rolled over her, she would have lived."

That's what I thought. Again, the fresh wound to my parental pride was grazed and my irritation with the suspicions of the local hospital's emergency room staff was aroused. It *wasn't* as bad as they had made it out to be. They weren't paying attention. They were on a witch hunt, and I was the one they were willing to burn at the stake.

I had loved that ER when Mighty Joe had been there. When he was beginning the fight for his life in that emergency room, the enterovirus was the enemy. But with Annesley, I had been the presumed enemy.

In contrast, when I checked Annesley in at Valley Children's Hospital for that follow-up visit six weeks later, the friendly, grand-motherly nurse took our names, glanced at her chart, and dramatically gasped. "Oh, Honey!" she said as she looked me straight in the eye. "Oh, I'm so sorry! What a horrible experience to have to live through!" Huh.

How could I be seen as the enemy in one medical facility but in another I was pitied as a mother who had been to the edge of despair? I felt entirely vindicated.

But really, why did that matter? It only mattered because I was still bowing down to my ugly idols of identity; I still wasn't seeing what God wanted me to see. It only mattered because I was looking to man to validate me. Powerful idol, isn't it? I was on a pendulum swing, from being the pitied victim with a brain-injured baby to being viewed as an atrocious mother who wanted to run over her child with a massive vehicle, and who must secretly feel foiled in that attempt.

If only I knew, beyond a shadow of a doubt, that my God is mightier than my Midianite army! Even if Joe had died, even if Annesley had been removed from our home—yes, even then—God is still good, still on the throne, still in control, still loves us, still fights for us, still has my back. Even then.

Even if I hadn't chosen to do all the "right" things. Even if I had gotten this whole parenting thing wrong. Even if all I had to offer him was my filthy sin and blatant failures. At that point, it was becoming clearer to me that really, that was all I had to offer anyway. The unmatched redemption of my life that Jesus had performed way back thousands of years was not just for the moment I realized I was saved but for *every single living moment of my life.*

I must battle Midianite armies the rest of my life. You must, too.

In the months that followed Annesley's accident, I was unreasonably afraid that something would happen to another of our children, forcing me once again to face a suspicious medical staff in an emergency room. What if one of the kids was jumping on the trampoline and broke an arm? "Child, get *out* of that tree!" I'd bellow across the backyard, picturing in my mind a forty-foot drop in slow motion.

I'm going to battle idols, and I'm going to battle my tendency to transfer my hope to those idolatrous things, looking for methods, theories, people, and things to do the saving that only God can do. It's my nature to drop my spear and go home, to shake like an Israelite when the blustering giant bellows his curses and threats across the land. I'll be the first one looking in the armory for a sturdy shield and spear before dropping to my knees, getting out of the way, and asking God to do his redemptive thing.

Author and mother Jodie Berndt writes in her book, *Praying the Scriptures for Your Children*:

> The sooner we realize that it is not about what we do but about what God does, the sooner we will stop focusing on ourselves and our shortcomings, and begin focusing on God and His power. Likewise, the sooner we quit worrying about doing our part, the sooner we can start rejoicing in the fact that God is doing His part. And the sooner we can recognize that God is at work, the sooner we can jump in and join Him.[4]

I would begin to learn it; I would gradually get closer. But not yet. Even now, as I realize that I still need to hear the gospel and live in it, I have to preach the gospel to myself every minute of every day.

"The LORD will fight for you, and you have only to be silent." (Exodus 14:14)

---

[4] Jodie Berndt, *Praying the Scriptures for Your Children* (Grand Rapids: Zondervan, 2013).

CHAPTER 8

One freezing cold January night, nearly eighteen months after Joe had battled the enterovirus and a year after Annesley's van accident, we met with a church leader whose counsel we had counted on in the past and whom we'd trusted during the years we'd spent entrenched in our religiosity. Our request to meet wasn't a surprise to him. After all, our lives had been turned inside out and back again through Mighty Joe's ordeal and Annesley's, too. And we were starting to realize that God was illuminating the path back to finding him.

Our life's tsunami had unsettled everything, but it was too late to turn around, now that we found ourselves falling in love with the Savior all over again. The chains of religious bondage were corroding, and the desire to bask in the simplicity of the gospel and say "Yes, Lord—more of you, less of me!" was growing into a faith that resembled the fire of our first love. We were back to when we knew the gospel and relied upon it, back to knowing Jesus trumped our security in our theology, back to the Holy Spirit who had drawn us in and lavished the limitless love of God upon us. Those elements of our faith had been missing for a painfully long time. We wondered, how had we gotten so lost?

So we sat in that coffee shop with our friend on that freezing winter night, our hands cupped around paper coffee mugs, the distinct sounds of bean grinders and milk steamers humming steadily from behind the counter.

"What is the problem?" he tentatively began, already with a half-sigh in his voice. He sounded particularly weary that evening, but we knew him to be a man who would kindly listen to what we had to say, even if he wouldn't agree. At the very least, we knew we had his ear for that evening, but it was likely he wasn't prepared to weather what we had to say.

"We feel that there's an increasing presence of legalistic practices and rigidity in this church, and judgment upon those of us who cannot agree with the lists of do's and don'ts anymore," we began. "We're starving for the gospel. Can we just preach the gospel?" Fletch implored. "Please. Less of what we must do, more of what Jesus did. The law never motivates anyone, but the gospel, grace, the love of God—that's the only thing that will light a fire within our sleepy and rebellious hearts."

Our friend acknowledged the gospel, and then I began to tell the story of the young girl brought into the PICU to die. I began to describe her death and her mother's sorrowful wailing outside Joe's room. To this day I cannot tell that story without tearing up and finding a catch in my throat as the emotion sweeps over me. I looked this man in the eye and said, "We need to be giving people the hope of the gospel! It's all about Jesus!"

He had been nodding his head as I told my story, eyes down, listening politely. But nothing really could have prepared me for his response. "Well," he answered evenly, "when we say it's all about Jesus, we're forgetting that Paul tells us clearly that we are to work out our salvation. There are many commandments we neglect when we say it's all about Jesus. We run the risk of becoming a church like ____," he named a big church in town that had once been given the deadly moniker of "Seeker-Sensitive" by those of us who were doing church "right."

Self-righteousness tells us that it's not all about Jesus, that there is something we all must do—as if we could. We attempt to attain some sort of "better righteousness" for ourselves, because despite our declarations of "Jesus alone" and "Grace alone" and "Faith alone," despite all five Solas of the Reformation, we turn to ourselves to gain some sort of righteousness that what—trumps Christ's? Adds to what he has already accomplished?

What did it mean when Jesus said, "It is finished"? And what does it actually mean when Paul tells us we are to work out our salvation?

The verses about working out our salvation are found in Paul's letter to the Philippians:

> Therefore, my beloved, as you have always obeyed, so now, not only as in my presence but much more in my absence, work out your own salvation with fear and trembling, for it is God who works in you, both to will and to work for his good pleasure. (Philippians 2:12–13)

The passage begins with the word *therefore*, which should always make us wonder what was said immediately prior to it (what's it "there for"?). What prompted Paul to introduce this command with the word *therefore*?

Verses 5 through 11 give the key:

> Have this mind among yourselves, which is yours in Christ Jesus, who, though he was in the form of God, did not count equality with God a thing to be grasped, but made himself nothing, taking the form of a servant, being born in the likeness of men. And being found in human form, he humbled himself by becoming obedient to the point of death, even death on a cross. Therefore God has highly exalted him and bestowed on him the name that is above every name, so that at the name of Jesus every knee should bow, in heaven and on earth and under the earth, and every tongue confess that Jesus Christ is Lord, to the glory of God the Father.

Jesus humbled himself to the extent of putting his earthly flesh to death for our sake, and we are to imitate his humility and service to others. But guess what? I can't muster up the strength to be humble. Much as I try, I can't just up and decide to be humble. We *can't* whip ourselves into humility as the monks of old sought to do. We can't hope to be more humble, and we can't will ourselves to be humble either. We can be like Christ only because he has made us like himself. We are already like Christ; now we are to live up to our status.

It's *his work*, not ours. At the very beginning of each of our salvation stories is God. Whether you're a Reformed theologian or a dyed-in-the-wool Arminian, the fact is that you were dead in your trespasses, and nothing breathes life into dry, dead bones but God himself.

Who does the redeeming and the restoring? God. Who paid for our fallenness? Jesus. He didn't "kind of" do it or leave some of it for us to finish up. He said, "It is finished," and it is.

Where did we get the notion that we had to do the work of making ourselves like Jesus? Where did we go so far off track as to think it's not all about him and that the *therefore* means that we must now get to work and start acting like Christians?

I don't want to "act like a Christian." There are plenty of hapless people filling up churches all over the world who think they're acting like Christians. I want to be reminded, every day, every hour, of what Jesus did for me—past tense—and of what he's doing for me presently. In that remembrance is the transforming power of grace and the crushing death of sin that *God works out for me.*

I will wrestle with sin until the day I die, but all along the way God is actively working in my life to crush my sin so that I become, day by day, year by year, more like Jesus. It's all about Jesus.

Because Jesus died for me, put an end to all my sin, and now lives for me, holy change is possible in my life. Yes, it matters how I live, but how I live is a generous and sovereign outpouring of the grace and work of God, not of me. Not of you. ". . . It is God who works in you, both to will and to work for his good pleasure" (Philippians 2:13).

There it is! God works in us, and I praise him for telling us that his work in us is what gives us the will to be like him. There's no ultimatum here, no pronouncement of "You'd better get your act together and quick, or you're in deep trouble." Neither is there a tedious list of do's and don'ts. Being like Jesus means being humble, contrite, and lovely. Being like Jesus means that God is laboring in your life and mine, working for his good pleasure. Being like Jesus means that all of that fruit of the Spirit so beautifully laid out in Galatians 5:22–23 is the result of Christ's work in me, beginning with Christ's work on the cross on my behalf. It's a finished work there, graciously continued by him in me, but not mustered up by me. I spent too many years trying to have the fruit of the Spirit, trying to be loving, joyful, peaceful, patient, kind, good, faithful, gentle, and self-controlled, but it wasn't until he showed me how to give up and give over my will to him that the fruit began to grow. He grabbed me, pulled me up out of the miry clay, as it were (that's a verse from Psalm 40), and gave me firm ground to stand upon. Oh! That's the deep, deep love of Jesus!

My thoughts often take me back to that somber night when the fragile young woman was brought to the PICU to die. I cannot know what dreadful grief her family still suffers today. I do not even know what her name was or where she lived or what she liked to do before she became so sick. But I will always remember her story as the turning point in our own, and I will always be grateful that God took that night and allowed it to be the beginning of our hope and freedom.

As Fletch and I sat in the coffee shop with our friend from church that January night, we couldn't know that we were just a week away from finding ourselves once again in an emergency room, standing over a gravely ill child. Yet another skilled surgeon would be informing us that our child could die within the hour. More unforeseen, draining weeks of a little life hanging in the balance lay ahead.

As we sat round that small table, sipping hot coffee and chai, we couldn't know how our struggles with our church practices would further ostracize us and push us ever closer to the cross. We thought we were about as shunned as we could be, but as God cast off more shackles and took us through the refining fire of a deadly illness once again, the pain of rejection and the sting of judgment just weren't as terrible as we might once have feared. Jesus was there in our trial, calling us, and doing his work of redemption.

Creation, fall, redemption—we were beginning to understand. What we hadn't known or expected was the realization that we were so lost, and that God was going to show us himself again. God is in the business of rebuilding and restoring broken lives, offering bitter water with healing properties, sweetening it with branches that bring life to parched, weary, broken, and dead souls. Religious souls. Religious souls like ours, stuck in the fall of our own creation story and now finding the redemption and restoration that only Jesus gives.

Had we known there would be healing in our future, we would have signed up for the trials a long time before.

CHAPTER 9

When people use the expression, "I feel like I'm in a fog," I often wonder if they've been in central California in the winter, in this agricultural valley where the Tule fog settles in with such density that you truly cannot see ten feet past your front door.

I remember my parents forbidding my older brother to leave the house one January evening to pick up a date because the fog was so thick that we couldn't see the street in front of our house! It's a thick, eerie fog, typically described by local weather forecasters as "blanketing the valley" and "pea soup"; impenetrable enough to keep a high school boy from taking a girl out for a soda on a Friday night.

Admittedly, my summer-loving personality struggles through the foggy season, and it's not unusual for us to grab all the kids and jump into the van, heading for the clear coast on a quest for sun, belting Jimmy Buffett's "Boat Drinks" loudly as the car drives out of the valley and the fog disappears in our wake.

It had been a full year since Annesley's accident with the van, and we had resumed the routine we knew so well: teens in and out, kids hunkered down over math books, and the washing machine steadily turning out load after load after load. Except we weren't "us" anymore. We were feeling unsettled, uneasy, and we knew that our lives were being met with growing suspicion by the people we had long considered our community. Of course, it wasn't one-sided. We had doubts and concerns of our own that we had started to voice.

Every social, educational, and spiritual choice our older kids made was now up for group discussion, typically behind our backs but occasionally lobbed with full-frontal skepticism. Two of our sons and a lifelong friend wanted to help lead worship during the all-church Sunday school time, so they asked us to help them write up a list of songs they knew would be acceptable. They practiced them like men on a mission and presented them to a couple of elders in charge of worship music. These young guys were excited by the possibility of using their gifts. Two of them play the guitar well; one sings and had been learning to lead. For inexperienced teens, they were doing a good job with their music.

I remember the day the men came to our home to meet with the boys who wanted to be a part of the fledgling music ministry, if you could call it that. Admittedly, the boys were proposing something new. Typically in our worship services, guitars were barely allowed; the piano was about the only approved instrument. I was washing dishes in the kitchen but could overhear some of their conversation, including the men's query, "So, what's your motive?"

Motive? I claim no particular expertise on teenagers, but as the mother of five teens, I'll tell you that often the motive is simple pleasure. It's no great secret that the pursuit of ungodly pleasure is what gets so many teens—and adults—into so much trouble. However, as an adult, lifelong follower of Jesus, I think the pursuit of godly pleasure is an *excellent* motive!

Just think of Eric Liddell, Olympic gold medalist and missionary to China, who was portrayed in the movie *Chariots of Fire* as remarking, "I believe that God made me for a purpose, but he also made me fast. When I run, I feel his pleasure." Yes! When we are using the gifts that God has given us, when we're serving him because we've been obedient to something he's nudged us to do, we'll feel his pleasure. And if others' motives are wrong or misplaced, we can trust the Holy Spirit to effect change in their hearts, for his glory—no skeptical questioning necessary.

We were becoming more and more uneasy. We soon realized that God was moving us out of the little church we had so painstakingly helped to build. Better, though, was the fact that he was deliberately, rapidly replacing our love for the church and our theology, platforms, and traditions with a deep love for him. Just him.[5]

And so we found ourselves in the middle of another bleak winter. Once again the fog was as thick as foam insulation and the trees were bare, with their silvery branches poking straight up, and the grass shimmering with frost in the early mornings. It was flu weather, and we all, one by one, had caught it.

A child gets sick and the house quiets down. A mother gets sick and the house slows to a crawl. The whole family gets sick and the house shuts down. All activity ceases, except for going about the business of being ill and caring for the sick.

Little makeshift sickbeds are made on bathroom floors so little people who aren't yet aware of what it means to get themselves to the toilet on time can throw up on the tile floor, which can be cleaned up with a stack of old towels. Daddy and Mommy are sleeping in the next room, so that little ones who are crying or in need of a glass of water can be easily heard in the middle of the night. In all our years of parenting a household of so many, a flu attack on all of us simultaneously has happened only twice. This was the year we were going to wish that winter had broken into an early spring.

Our very girly, brown-haired, blue-eyed Caroline was eight years old that January. Like the rest of us, she was down for the count with a stomach virus that seemed to hit her worse than anyone else. While the rest of us began to recover, she slept for hours at a time, and she wasn't interested in the saltine crackers, applesauce, and bubbly ginger ale we offered. She slept on a bed made of rag towels arranged carefully on her bathroom floor. She hardly moved during the day, so I walked her to my bedroom one afternoon to watch some television. I hoped to lift her spirits in a cheery room filled with sunlight streaming through the plantation shutters and a fire in the fireplace.

---

[5] And though I am getting ahead of the story, we eventually did leave this church and joined another. We would badly need a place to heal.

"My stomach hurts, Mommy."

"I know, Baby. Mine does too. That's what happens when you throw up a lot. Your stomach hurts."

I made her protein shakes with yogurt, hoping to give her strength to fight whatever was bringing her down and cheering on those little probiotics to do their clever thing in her gut. She took a measly sip.

I rallied the recovering troops and escorted them to my bedroom as I announced, "Let's have a 'See who can make Caroline laugh' contest!"

One by one, willing sisters and brothers did their best to make funny faces, tell her jokes they knew she loved, and dance in the goofiest way possible. Caroline never cracked a smile and was notably, uncharacteristically annoyed that we were blocking her view of the television.

That evening, Fletch arrived home, having completed the last day of his workweek, rightfully concerned that Caroline was still not recovering and still responding with increasing disinterest in getting herself healthy. Like most kids, ours have had times of "convenient" sickness, only to recover miraculously when told that their brothers and sisters are outside swimming or that a grandparent is planning to visit.

In those moments of irony, I'm always reminded of Shel Silverstein's pint-sized hypochondriac, Peggy Ann McKay:

"I cannot go to school today,"
Said little Peggy Ann McKay.
"I have the measles and the mumps
A gash, a rash, and purple bumps."[6]

The poem goes on to describe little Peggy's many afflictions, from chicken pox to numb toes to a shrunken brain. One by one, Peggy painstakingly lists her maladies until finally, she says:

---

[6] Shel Silverstein, *Where the Sidewalk Ends* (New York: HarperCollins, 2014).

"I have a hangnail, and my heart is—what?
What's that? What's that you say?
You say today is . . . Saturday?
G'bye, I'm going out to play!"

This is normal kid behavior. It's a signal that the child is on the mend and ready to be up and about, because if she's really under the weather, she'll happily stick to the sofa with her blankie and a third viewing of *The Lion King*.

Caroline wasn't pretending, and she wasn't getting any better. In fact, that Thursday evening she seemed to be getting worse.

Dehydration? Highly possible. We had taken her to our family doctor several years back when she had become a little spacey and couldn't tell us her name. He had recognized her symptoms, all pointing to dehydration. Fletch had administered small sips of water, and soon she was skipping around the driveway, the bright and exuberant little girl we always knew her to be.

But this time, there was no happiness or turnaround when her daddy tried to make her drink water. It was getting late, and she was very sleepy, so we made her a comfy bed of blankets and had her lie down in our bathroom so that we could keep a closer eye on her. Fletch took her temperature but found it to be a benchmark 98°, nothing to cause panic. Still concerned, Fletch told me he would take her to the emergency room if she wasn't better in the morning.

CHAPTER 10

Caroline wasn't better in the morning. She was spacey, just as she had been when she was dehydrated. Her skin was mottled, weird, and clammy. My heart started racing and I began to talk to her in a rapid series of questions, trying to get her to respond, attempting to make her understand that we needed to get her to the hospital.

As I carefully slipped flip-flops onto her feet and pulled a sweatshirt over her jammie pants, Fletch was dialing a family friend, an emergency room physician and a dad of lots of his own little ones. He had become the head of the ER where both Joe and Annesley had initially been cared for before their transfers to Valley Children's. Dr. William Clark was working on the computer in his kitchen that morning, munching down breakfast and wrapping up a few details before leaving for his shift.

"She's not well, William. We're bringing her in. Will you be there?"

William was as alarmed as we were, having discerned from Fletch's description that Caroline was in a precarious position and needed to be seen immediately. "I'll meet you there!" he replied. Both men hung up their phones and the race to the emergency room was underway.

As we drove through drizzling rain, over the railroad tracks that separate our country town from the city beyond, we prayed that there would be no train to hinder our progress. By the time we arrived at the hospital, William was standing outside at the corner of the building, scanning the parking lot, waiting with a wheelchair for Caroline. He spotted us pulling in and dashed toward our van. Helping Caroline into the chair, we all moved as quickly as possible into the emergency room, through the bustling waiting area, past triage and a confused contingent of nurses. As we flew past them, William called out, "She's very sick!" I remember that we moved as a single, blurred unit, pushing the wheelchair, plowing through the white double doors that whooshed shut behind us.

In mere seconds, William and a waiting nurse had Caroline on the emergency gurney in the trauma unit, temperature taken, and prepped for a CT, as efficient as a pit crew on race day.

"I'm almost certain it's a ruptured appendix," William told us. "All of her symptoms are pointing to it. At the very least it's appendicitis. Either way, we'll have to get it out of there as quickly as we can. Her system is shutting down."

Caroline was oblivious to the flurry of activity that surrounded her. As minute IV lines were inserted into her veins and her clothes were replaced with a surgical gown, she murmured sleepily and closed her eyes, content to have Dr. Clark speak words of calm assurance into her ear. Then she was off to be scanned, with careful attention being paid to what else might be going on inside that little body. In such a precarious situation, scans are read quickly, and hers showed exactly what Dr. Clark knew in his heart: Caroline's appendix had ruptured and infection was filling her body, shutting her systems down, and sending her into septic shock.

We were left standing in the trauma room. Waiting. Wondering. Once again praying for the technicians and medical staff. Texting friends and grandparents. Posting updates to Facebook.

Guilt. Disbelief. How did we miss this? A ruptured appendix!

"Oh, Honey!" said one nurse as she reassuringly rubbed my arm. "Ruptured appendixes can be very difficult to detect. Your whole family was sick, weren't they? That makes perfect sense! When you're all feeling lousy and aching from the pain, no one's illness stands out. In fact, the same thing happened to a nurse's daughter here last year. Talk about guilt!"

Thank you, God. Thank you for sending the best, most soothing words at exactly the right moment.

But I was again missing the point, wasn't I? In my panicked thoughts of, *What will they think?* and *How did this happen?* I was again forgetting that my identity was firmly planted in Christ. He had my back. In that same emergency room where I was treated as a suspect in the van accident with Annesley, I was once again shifting my hope to my reputation and away from the One who had given everything he had for me.

I had, again, forgotten the gospel.

Here, once more, in the same trauma unit where we were told Mighty Joe needed a transfer and could die on the way to Children's Hospital, a surgeon was informing us of the risk posed to Caroline's life: "Your daughter is very sick." Surgeon Dr. Tam spoke with authority and the easy confidence that comes with experience. "With an infection like this, there's always a chance that she could have a heart attack and die while we're in there."

We nodded to acknowledge his warning. We're not the type of parents to break down in the face of trouble; we had so many reasons to trust that God had Caroline's best in mind. If she lived or died on that operating table, we knew, we trusted, that God had a purpose that was for our good.

> For I know the plans I have for you, declares the LORD, plans for welfare and not for evil, to give you a future and a hope. Then you will call upon me and come and pray to me, and I will hear you. You will seek me and find me, when you seek me with all your heart. I will be found by you, declares the LORD. . . . (Jeremiah 29:11–14a)

We have to ask ourselves even in the most pressing moments, *Do we believe him or don't we?*

An hour later, we were staring out the windows of the operating room waiting area into the gray sky, happy to see my parents walk in to offer understanding hugs and undying support. They had been several hours down the road on their way to southern California when we called with the news that we were, yet again, in the emergency room with yet another child. My father's placid reserve serves him well in these moments, and his tranquil response on the phone had transferred a sense of calm all the way to me.

When I was a small child, the treasured teenage daughter of friends was killed in a car accident, and my father was asked to break the news to her five siblings. Over my lifetime I've seen him called into service in such situations because he can detach himself from the emotion and chaos surrounding such a crushing event to relay what needs to be communicated. In a crisis, during those dark periods when we can't see what's to our left or our right, when our blurred vision has us feeling like life is one long winter in the fog, it is evidence of God's grace and mercy when he sends us people who can speak his peace over us like a healing balm.

When my mother told my father that she wanted to turn around and head back up to northern California and be with us, my father didn't hesitate to change their plans. And there they were, praying with us, waiting the hours out, trusting that the God who formed Caroline in my womb would show his mighty hand whether she lived or died that day.

Prayers, waiting, nervous laughter, trivial conversation. We would check the time on our phones, check the texts coming in, check the weather, check Facebook, check Twitter, check anything to fill the time as we waited in that room overflowing with people also awaiting news of their loved ones. The lady at the desk would call out names when there was news to share. At the slightest sound of her voice, the room would immediately fall silent.

It seemed an achingly long time before our names were called. "Parents of Caroline Fletcher." We never knew we could get up from our chairs so quickly. We were ushered into a hallway to wait, again, for the surgeon to meet us with news.

What was going on? They called our names but there we stood, the four of us, silent. "It must be bad. They wouldn't have called our names so soon if the news was good."

Oh God! What if she had died on the operating table? Oh God. Oh God of the universe, Lover of our souls, Creator of the stars and the moon and every hair on Caroline's head. God! My mind raced, then slowed to a screeching halt. It sped toward disaster like a tornado, grabbing every extraneous speculation, and then stalled like a sputtering engine, faltering, failing, blank.

I plopped heavily onto a bench; I stood back up. I switched places with my mom; my dad rubbed my back; Fletch told me I was jumping to conclusions that weren't necessarily the truth.

And then Dr. Tam came through the door.

"Sorry to keep you waiting. She was very sick. We were able to remove the appendix in about fifteen minutes, but it took us forty-five minutes to clean her abdominal cavity. There was pus surrounding her organs, and we don't think we got it all. It's likely we'll have to place drains if the medications don't hit the infection soon. But she's doing great, and as soon as we get her comfortable in the ICU, you can see her."

It took every scrap of self-control I had to not throw my arms around this man and hug him. Grateful. Relieved.

We made our way to the elevators and rode up to the floor that housed the ICU, catching Caroline being wheeled in just before the heavy doors shut. She looked as if she'd been struck by lightning, her hair all disheveled and her eyes sleepily half-shut. She was intubated—not what a mama wants to see—but as she began to come out of the anesthesia she gazed up at us and mouthed the words: "I feel fine. I want to go home."

Home. So did we. Home was just a weekend away.

CHAPTER 11

Sunday morning. We'd now hit the fourth day in the ICU, and it was painfully obvious that no one was going home anytime soon.

"Caroline, Honey, you need to get up and walk today. Do you think you can do that? Come on. Up we go. We need to get you walking."

The end of the hallway was at most 200 feet, but my girl was already whimpering. "I can't do this," she moaned. "Please, Mommy, don't make me walk!"

Each step was labored. My half-grown daughter moved like a hunched-over little old woman, inching her way along the hall on feet too short to hold her frame. Every shuffle away from the bed and toward the passageway came with weeping, with exaggerated and uncharacteristic complaining. *How* many steps to make it to her door? Ten? Twenty? Too many.

Her moods matched the gray sky: cold toward us, combative toward nurses, uncooperative if her day required anything but sleep and staring at the television. In my gut, I knew this wasn't my Caroline, my Sweet Caroline, but in the pressure of a situation where I felt helpless, uninformed, and educationally inferior to the medical personnel, I didn't have the confidence to insist that something was still seriously wrong with her.

Nurses seemed to understand and listen to my concerns; the doctor on call for the weekend did not. "Look, I know you want to make things easy for your child, but you have to make her do her breathing exercises or she's going to develop pneumonia. Do you understand me?"

He was in my face, challenging me, making judgment calls about my parenting (over which he had no authority), telling me that Caroline wasn't trying hard enough with her incentive spirometer breathing measurement or putting out enough effort to walk the hallway. And it was my fault. *My* fault?

Again, the doubts arose within me. I knew this behavior wasn't normal for my Caroline, and yet, I'm not a doctor, so what do I know? We pushed her harder. Fletch made little tissue paper ghosts and tied them to strings that dangled from her IV pole so she could blow her breaths out harder and make them "fly." We bribed her with movies and Popsicles and visits from sisters to get her to take more steps and walk farther.

But we weren't the only ones with doubts. Caroline had two nurses named Kelly; one was consistently on a day shift and the other on the night shift, so we called them "Day Kelly" and "Night Kelly." Both quietly expressed concern about how Caroline was responding.

On the day I was scolded by the doctor on call, a no-nonsense charge nurse gave me a glance that made me think she may have some thoughts on the matter. I knew she wouldn't directly challenge a doctor's opinion, but I valued her perspective.

"If Caroline were your child," I proposed, "would you push her harder or demand that more medical tests be run to see if something else was going on?" She looked at her clipboard, wrote something down, then responded without lifting her eyes to meet mine. "If she were my child . . ." and then shook her head. She wanted to answer that she would have pushed the doctor for more.

At this point, doing things the way we had all weekend, we weren't making any progress, so Fletch decided it was time to start making some noise. However, the surgeon who had performed Caroline's appendectomy had gone out of town on vacation, and the doctor on call wasn't willing to order another scan. Looking back, we think he didn't want to make a decision in the absence of the other surgeon. Meanwhile, Caroline wasn't recovering, the infection was lingering, and we were biding our time. Had the doctor on call explained his hesitation, things could have gone differently, but he didn't do anything. Nothing.

Hmmph.

In the midst of such unsettling predicaments, God is still God. He is still on the throne. He's not surprised, not sitting up in heaven thinking, *Oh, oh. What shall we do? How am I going to get the surgeon to make the right decision for Caroline?* Yet we often question, wonder, and speculate, *What is God doing? If only he would reveal his strategy to me plainly. If only.*

"I will never leave you nor forsake you," God has promised. "So we can confidently say, 'The Lord is my helper; I will not fear; what can man do to me?'" (Hebrews 13:5–6). These shaky moments of doubt and fear are dynamic hope tests. First we think, *If only [this thing] would happen, then all will be right with my world.* These unwonted (and perhaps often unwanted?) experiences thrust us back into a conflict, revealing where our hope really lies.

Remember the grand story of Scripture we touched on when this story was about Mighty Joe? The great big story line of Scripture is creation, fall, redemption, restoration. Was I now remembering that there would be redemption in Caroline's story, too? Where was my hope that day in the hospital hallway when an insensitive surgeon barked at me? Was I trusting in the surgeon, in his decisions, in the hospital personnel, in my husband's determination to push them all to formulate a better plan for Caroline? Or was I believing that the God who had so painstakingly and perfectly formed her tiny person inside my womb (creation) and allowed her body to become so severely ill (fall) had already crafted a master plan to pull her out of the depths of her despair (redemption) and then completely restore her, even if it meant her restoration was not here, but in heaven?

As it happened, enough noise was made about Caroline's lack of recovery among the ICU staff that a scan was ordered. She was soon on her way to a second surgery. The doctor and technicians quickly discovered that infection was indeed still hiding in the deep, far pockets of her abdomen, as thick as pancake batter. The substitute surgeon was requiring her to walk when the pus made it excruciating to simply breathe.

The drain placement procedure involved placing a drain inside her abdomen, with the hand of the surgeon guided by a CT scan just above her, searching her middle on the operating table. It wasn't particularly dangerous, but she did have to be put under anesthesia once more.

When Fletch was a newly graduated dentist, he worked in a dental office that specialized in treating children. They often called in an anesthesiologist for cases that required sedation and, while these cases became somewhat commonplace for Fletch, they were difficult for me to see.

One afternoon I had dropped by the dental office, and as I rounded the corridor into the operatory where patients recovered from surgery, I was stopped dead in my tracks at the sight of a small, sweet boy who looked to me in every way to be dead. He lay on a dental chair far too large for his spindly little frame, head cocked to one side, a breathing tube protruding from his mouth and not a muscle engaged from head to toe. I gasped! It took me several seconds to realize that he was under anesthesia and very much alive, but it jarred me that day and I knew I never wanted to see a child of mine in such a condition.

And yet there Caroline was: unresponsive, relaxed in an other-worldly way, tube extruding from her mouth and hair flayed behind her on the low vinyl table. Fletch stayed at her side, holding her hand and stroking her hair, but I could not. I could only lean my weak self against the wall outside the operating room and pray.

Lord, you know why. I was often at a loss for words to offer upwards. Tired—so bone weary.

"She's fine," Fletch was soon saying, his arm around my shoulders to pull me close. "They placed the drain and it should be doing its job now. She'll be out of the woods and on her way home soon."

Nonetheless, just a few days later, we were beginning week two and things were still not going the way we had hoped. We were deeply exhausted, and our ability to cope with Caroline's wild mood swings and sluggish recovery had waned. I did my crying at home so that I could return to the hospital with a chipper attitude and an ounce of hope.

One afternoon Caroline asked for a Popsicle. We were encouraged by her desire for something to eat, and the list of flavor options was rapidly produced. Caroline chose "blue."

Several minutes later, a nurse entered the room and gasped, flying toward the bed to put her face right up to Caroline's. "Oh!" she began to laugh. "Oh! You had me panicking for a minute there! All I could see from the door were your blue lips and I thought, 'Holy cow! Someone get this kid some oxygen!'" You can be sure Caroline asked for another blue Popsicle the next day, just to see if she could freak out anyone else.

After the drain placement surgery, no one was seeing the improvement we were hoping it would provide. She was not better. The insidious pus remained, deep down in a cavity that would require more meticulous precision than the surgeons were initially willing to devote. We wouldn't be going home soon, and somewhere, somehow, we needed to understand that Caroline's "grand story" included the rendering of the gospel over our lives in a fresh way. We would comprehend the redemption and restoration of this story someday, but not until we had experienced a number of discouraging days that drove us into the lowest depths of our fall.

CHAPTER 12

The rain. The unrelenting rain. Big fat plunky drops chased me as I ran from the hospital parking lot, zig-zagging past service trucks, hatchbacks, and motorcycles, and cutting across the planter strip, dashing to the sidewalk. I shook the rain off my sweatshirt right outside the big electric doors, my shoes squeaking and my toes already icy cold. At this point it all just felt like a movie, as if we had ordered weather to match our mood.

Another drain needed to be positioned deep past Caroline's abdomen and into her pelvis, but this time the surgery would be extremely delicate. The abdominal aorta splits into the internal and external iliac arteries as they enter the pelvis. Because the abdominal aorta is the largest in the body, puncturing it can lead to catastrophic bleeding.

Two well-qualified vascular surgeons debated the merits of one approach or another—two surgeons playing Rock-Paper-Scissors to see who might be able to walk away from the responsibility. Their haggling took a full day. Caroline languished, still unwilling to walk the ICU hallway, still lashing out at nurses when her pain meds took a dive, still playing her blue Popsicle joke on any hapless victim she could fool.

"We have to thread the drain tube carefully, because if we are off by mere millimeters, we could puncture the abdominal aorta and she'll bleed out." Not really reassuring.

We sent out texts and prayer requests; faithful friends were once again called upon to lift our requests before the throne of grace as they interceded on tireless knees. My best friend Lisa, devotedly by my side during every one of these crises, sat and chatted with Fletch while I ran a necessary errand. She and I had been friends since college, and bridesmaids in each other's weddings. We had walked the long, colorful journeys of our lives together ever since. Their laughter was the last thing I heard as I left to run out to the drugstore.

I returned, hoping that the whole thing would be over. Amid the prolonged deliberations of those two doctors, I had not exactly come away feeling confident. Was my hope shifting again? This seems to be a deeply embedded pattern. If I had been hoping in what the surgeons could perform, my hope was again (again!) sorely misplaced.

I'm reminded of the Israelites after God delivered them from hundreds of years of slavery in Egypt. When they realized the challenges that lay ahead of them on their way to the Promised Land, you might be amazed to learn that one of the first things they pined away for was onions! They were shifting their hope back to the land of Egypt instead of to God himself and where he was taking them. But we're no different. It wasn't hundreds of years for us; it was eighteen months filled with a trio of children's calamities, during which we had placed our hope in . . . what?

Us. *Our* goodness. *Our* lack of goodness. *Our* performance. *Our* choices. *Our* circumstances. The doctors. The nurses. The medications. The recovery period. Nutrition.

"Everything looks great," the surgeon was saying. "We slid the drain straight in there, and it should pull out everything that's remaining. Once we can get her cleaned out, she should be on the road to recovery."

Oh, sweet words to hear! Sweet words that made us hopeful, despite the fact that Caroline would continue to fight us over the next ten days, not happy, not wanting to eat, not keeping anything down at all.

Her stubborn resistance to food was keeping us all stuck, spinning our wheels. If she ate to Dr. Tam's satisfaction, she could go home, but she refused, fearful of the pain and vomiting that might ensue once solid food met her lips.

Nineteen days after Caroline's body went into septic shock and all of this began, I found myself on a lonely road one afternoon, driving home alongside the railroad tracks and past the cemetery. I was overwhelmed with a fatigue born out of sleepless nights on an uncomfortable hospital chair with the noises of intensive care all around me. I began to sob, my shoulders heaving up and down and tears flowing off my cheeks and onto my hands as they gripped the steering wheel.

"God, I don't understand it! I know you have this under control, but I cannot see how we are going to dig ourselves out of this black hole! If she eats, she can go home, but every time she eats, she vomits. And round and round and round."

Once home, my emotionally charged soliloquy continued as I locked myself in my bathroom and turned on the shower to drown out my weeping. This wasn't what I wanted. This, a third time. "What's the point of prayer," I prayed, "if you're just going to do what you have already planned anyway?"

Unlike me, God is gracious. At that point, amid the despair and lassitude that had overcome my worn-out, feeble frame, he whispered in my ear, "I am your hope." Author Elyse Fitzpatrick reminds me, "For every time I've stamped my foot and said, 'This isn't what I want!' the Father hears the Son's 'Not my will but Thine' instead." The gracious God who had watched me try to find my worth in what I had crafted by my own hands, looking for redemption in the things we had chosen for our family, now graciously, gently nudged us through near-tragedies so that he could say those words and have them heard by now-tender hearts: "I am your hope."

That gracious God is our hope—that God looks at us in the midst our foot-stamping tantrums and sees Jesus there, hands and feet splayed, nailed to a wooden cross, instead.

On day twenty-one, Caroline ate. A humble bean and cheese burrito pulled her out of her slump, and by afternoon, discharge orders were making the rounds. No one wanted to keep her on that recovery floor a day longer, and Dr. Tam knew she'd recuperate more quickly at home.

Our last hospital hours were on a rainy Thursday evening. One set of grandparents was there for a surprise visit; the other set of grandparents was at home waiting to welcome us, and into the car went our weak but happy girl.

If I were to tell you that our seventh child had a febrile seizure just two days later, would you believe me? There, rubbing his little back while he slowly revived, I looked upwards and yelled, "Uncle!" We were exhausted, of course, and brought to the very end of ourselves.

It's easy to yell "Uncle!" and shake a fist at God. That's what we do when we can't see where God is taking us because our human view of our circumstances is puny and inadequate. The grand story here would read this way:

> Caroline is a healthy girl with no medical concerns (creation).
> Because of an undetected ruptured appendix, her body
> descends into septic shock, verging on death (fall). Through
> a series of painful surgeries and recovery, her life is spared
> (redemption). Out of her pain and the further refining
> of our lives—stripping us of our own resources—we are
> drawn, once again, to the beauty and simplicity of the gospel
> (restoration).

A funny thing happened on the way to recovery: we met Jesus all over again. With our lives ripped open, the Holy Spirit stepped in with power and authority, and we fell into the sheltering arms of our Savior. We knew then that we never, ever wanted to leave that place of refuge.

When our fall leads to redemption and our Redeemer begins his work of restoration, nothing is as sweet as sitting still. Staying put, allowing Jesus to consume us, letting go of our relentless pursuit of control, understanding, finally, that nothing in this world matters but him. His love, grace, and mercy are entirely irresistible, even though I know my default sin is to try to rely on myself all over again.

Call me simple. Call me gospel-focused. Call me unsophisticated, uneducated, unwilling to stray from the cross. Call me a lover of Jesus, a scoffer of religion, a girl who wants more of God, more of his Holy Spirit, more of him and far, far less of me. When he reminds me that my identity is in God alone, nothing else matters at all.

CHAPTER 13

Spring. New life, new hope, new vision. I placed the colorful plastic Resurrection eggs on the dining room table. Each contained a symbol that related to the last week of Christ's life before he was crucified: a tiny metal stake representing the nails driven through his hands, a piece of purple cloth to represent the purple robe that was put on Jesus while they were mocking him, and so on.

We were once more walking the little ones in our family through the resurrection story and teaching them why we celebrate Easter. Christmas is a joyful celebration in our home, but each year I long to make Easter bigger, more celebratory, and more enticing than the hoopla surrounding Christmas. The hope of Christ's death and resurrection and what it means for us—I want my kids to grow up rejoicing in the magnitude of that gift.

Caroline was slowly recovering. She napped most afternoons, and she ambled slowly from room to room, from couch to chair to bed. She bowed out of events she normally would have been enthusiastic about attending. We watched her carefully and provided the nourishing food and rest that recovery requires. Her brothers and sisters tenderly and gently interacted with her, and she responded with a gratitude that had not been there previously. Gradually, our lives were returning to whatever we thought normal was before all of this.

Fletch and I were emerging from our stunned, deer-in-the-headlights response to what had been thrown at us in other arenas as well. Truthfully, I hesitantly wondered what was coming next.

Which child would be found facedown in the pond or fallen from a tree to severely fracture a collarbone or wind up impaled by a pencil? Such were the wild irrational thoughts that would pass through my mind when the house grew still. My heart would race and my breaths would become shallow little gasps until the Holy Spirit nudged me to remember whose I am. That the Creator of the universe doesn't act randomly or unknowingly. That he has this, all of this.

As the thoughts would overtake me in the middle of the night, God also reminded me that there were untold blessings surrounding the circumstances of Joe's virus, Annesley's accident, and Caroline's illness. The gifts he gave us in the midst of chaos and loss are as stunning as the way in which he redeemed each tragedy.

Months after Mighty Joe had fought the enterovirus in Children's Hospital, I learned that a woman name Melinda, whom I had met only a couple of times, had come to the hospital to pray for us. She didn't know which motor home was ours (it had been lent to us by Fletch's generous parents), so she had walked the parking lot praying around *all* of the RVs parked there. Melinda had us covered in prayer when we were wholly unaware of her gift. I remain humbled and thankful for that woman of prayer, who knew we needed bolstering even when we were numbed by the tragedy we were facing.

The hospitalists assigned to Joe's case were our advocates from day one, and they tirelessly worked to solve the puzzle that proved to be the enterovirus. We often wondered if those two men ever saw their homes; it seemed to us that they were always present, always caring, always laboring on behalf of these terribly sick ones. I would look up from the work on my laptop to see Dr. Kallas standing outside Joe's room, eyeing him through the window, his massive, strong hand under his chin, thinking through the many problems that plagued our tiny man.

And my beautiful sister-in-law was working right there, always stopping in to see how Joe was doing and how we were doing. My parents, too, were just a few miles away, dropping in to do my laundry, stock the RV refrigerator, or bring our other kiddos for a visit.

On the morning when we discovered Caroline so near to system shutdown, Fletch's first thought was to call ER physician Dr. William Clark, who at the time was only an acquaintance. Will later told us that he normally would have been at work at the time Fletch called, but he happened to be sitting by the phone that day. As soon as their conversation ended, William had raced to the hospital, beating us there to meet us in the parking lot. His skill and knowledge played a significant role in saving Caroline's life.

A restaurateur and catering friend, who had watched his own daughter's life end abruptly in childhood because of a birth defect, reached out to us with an ice chest packed full of food. He knew the pain of our ordeal and the fright of watching your baby fade, and he ministered to us in a way that poured straight out of his heart.

Friends delivered care packages filled with snacks, books, Bible verses, lip balm, and sundry distractions. Friends of friends who didn't know us nevertheless sent notes of kindness, activities for Annesley's recovery, and balloons to cheer up Caroline in those ICU days that dragged on endlessly for her. The students, parents, and faculty of the Christian high school in the town where I grew up had Caroline on their prayer list day after day.

God loves us, and we were beginning to learn to live like we were loved.

My son, do not despise the LORD's discipline or be weary of his reproof, for the LORD reproves him whom he loves, as a father the son in whom he delights. (Proverbs 3:11–12)

Was it true? Could God really love us as the puffed-up, self-righteous Pharisees we had become? Even more, could he love us even if we didn't conform to the standards he holds or to our self-imposed markers of Christian living, such as homeschooling, correct theology, and certain styles of dress? Could it be that his grace and mercy were for the sinners we still were, and not just for the time when we first acknowledged our need for a Savior and began this walk of faith?

Remarkably, he loves us so much that he would allow a virus to attack the body of our precious baby, allow me to experience the horror of running over my own child with the injury that resulted, and allow me to see Caroline's body give out from a series of life-threatening events to her eight-year-old frame. "For the LORD reproves him whom he loves, as a father the son in whom he delights" (Proverbs 3:12). Oh, but those are mercies! That's how we are tested and made more like him!

Recently I was sitting on the beach with a friend, our toes wriggling deep into the sand, our backs against colorful sling-back chairs, and the scents of the ocean and suntan lotion wafting around us. We were soaking up the August sun and enjoying the peaceful crash of the Pacific Ocean as its powerful waves met the shoreline.

This is my favorite place on earth and I gain clarity here. I told my friend that I felt like I'd been given a new beginning, really. I'd spent forty years attempting some sort of sorry self-redemption, knowing academically that Jesus had paid it all and that he was my identity, but not living free and in his love enough to understand that my additional attempts were a futile exercise in self-help.

"You know me well enough and long enough now to know that I have always struggled with gossip," I quietly remarked to my beach friend.

"Yes," she replied, with that casual caution friends employ when the conversation turns toward self-reflection.

"It's gone. I don't want any part of it. I know that only Jesus could have done that, but I also know that it happened only because he showed me how to give up trying. I am learning to shut up and let him do his work in my life. Isn't that crazy?"

"It doesn't sound reasonable," she answered, "but the older I get, the more I understand that the law never motivates us to do anything, does it? Only the grace, mercy, and love of Jesus truly change us."

I was learning to live as one who is loved, and I was being changed. I am learning to meditate on the truth of Exodus 14:14, "The LORD will fight for you, and you have only to be silent." His work, not mine. His gentle guidance that leads me to repentance, heart change, and obedience, but not the other way around, which is what I was caught up in for so many years. Our obedience follows his grace, not the other way around.

Criticism of others, judgment of behaviors—these attributes once marked my character, but I have been freed. Those things still pop up and kick me in the rear when I least expect it, but I don't have to stay there. Secure in the love of God, I am free to love others as they are, where they are. I'm not perfect at it, but here's where I can say, "This is why I need Jesus!"

Living in the light of the gospel allows me to look at debauched humanity and say, "Oh! That wretched soul needs Jesus! Oh! How he's trying to find his worth and value in what others think, say, and do. He needs Jesus! She needs the good news!" Then I can take the light of the cross to those darkened corners to pour out Christ over them. The gospel doesn't ever allow us the snobbish luxury of not sullying our hands because we can't stand the filth. We are clean only because Christ is clean; they will be made clean only if we take Christ to them.

Let's free others to learn to live as if they too are loved, because they are. You are too.

EPILOGUE

In him you also, when you heard the word of truth,
the gospel of your salvation, and believed in him,
were sealed with the promised Holy Spirit.
—Ephesians 1:13

What defines you? Who gave you that definition? Think about your earliest years and how you defined or identified yourself then. Were you a soccer star? The class clown? Someone's son? What about now? When asked about yourself, do you immediately reply, "I'm a stockbroker" or "I'm just a stay-at-home mom"?

When Caroline turned ten, I took her on a mother-daughter retreat to celebrate her birthday. We made our way to a beautiful Christian retreat center nestled in the Santa Cruz Mountains, rolling our car windows down and breathing deeply the scents of pines and redwoods. We laughed together through tire swing rides, craft projects designed to delight young girls, and conversations with other mothers and daughters doing life together.

We gathered after dinner for the first group teaching time, little girls antsy in their chairs and moms thankful to have another godly voice speak into their lives. Right out of the gate, our speaker challenged the girls to think about their identity. Aha! We had been learning to rest in our identity in Christ, and this weekend would dovetail nicely.

The energetic young speaker threw out a question to the girls: "Who makes up your identity as you walk through life?" Little shouts of "family!" and church!" and "school!" were lobbed toward the front of the room, and I smiled to myself, thinking for sure our speaker would eventually emphasize that our identity lies in Christ alone. But she did not.

As Caroline and I sat on our sleeping bags that night, whispering and chatting about the day, I had to grab the opportunity to remind my daughter of her true identity. "Honey, when the speaker asked about our identity, what would you have answered if you had been given a chance?" She echoed the answers her peers gave earlier, and my heart sank a little.

"Sweetheart, your identity is not us. I want you to have wonderful memories of your childhood, and I want you to always love being a Fletcher, but Honey, your identity is never, never, never us. Your identity is Jesus, your Redeemer. Don't forget that. If you learn anything in our home, I want you to walk away knowing whose you are and what he has done for you."

In the lives my children will live, in the life I have ahead of me and you have ahead of you, only one identity is worth owning, because all of the others are merely descriptors. They can change minute by minute (now I've got my mom hat on, now my homeschool hat, now I'm Fletch's wife, now I'm a writer . . .), weekly, or yearly. The man with the thirty-year career in sales can have it ripped out from under him in a two-minute conversation with his boss, or a brief email appearing suddenly in an inbox.

That's what happened to Dr. William Clark, our emergency room physician who did so much for Caroline. He was the man who immediately jumped into action upon hearing Fletch's description of her symptoms over the phone, who met us in the hospital parking lot and wheeled Caroline back to prep her for surgery. His quick thinking played a major role in saving her life that day.

William had always taken the challenge to be better, go farther, work harder. The competitive environment of medical school appealed to his nature, a call to excellence in a field that would allow him to be in control of chaos.

There are few places where chaos reigns more regularly than in an ER, and William thrived in a frenetic emergency room that sees 75,000 patients per year. He became a board member, the medical director, and the go-to guy in the hospital where Mighty Joe, Annesley, and Caroline had seen the first leg of their care. We were deeply thankful for his presence that day in January 2010, when Caroline could have lost her life before we even arrived at the hospital.

Like me, like many of us, William had been taught that his identity was in Jesus, but he never had grasped the day-to-day reality of living there. To him, too, the gospel was the gateway, not necessarily the place where we dwell and certainly not the conduit that delivers a life of freedom, mercy, and grace.

Almost a year after Caroline's appendix ruptured, William's distinguished career as an emergency room physician was about to come to a screeching halt. An old injury deep and low in his spine was flaring up to a degree he could no longer ignore. Although William had undergone surgery for a herniated disk when he was in high school, it had never cured the problems that plagued him throughout his adult life. The stress of his job, stacking work shifts, and the busyness of his home life, where seven children arrived one right after another, began to take their toll. William found himself once again on the operating table, once more the patient, and decidedly not in control of the chaos.

After months of pushing himself through the pain, things were looking up. Just days out of surgery, William felt completely relieved of the pain that had been holding him back. Seven days of complete healing followed his surgery, seven days of believing life would resume as usual.

But it was not to be. William reported, "I was just walking by the foot of our bed and then—bam! Re-herniated the disk. I felt like I'd been hit by lightning."

William's surgeon wanted another MRI, but the image showed nothing. In the midst of the turmoil, William's mom suggested that he check out a church with a well-known healing ministry located about four miles from William's home. Admittedly skeptical, he dismissed her recommendation and instead headed for a third surgery on his herniated disk. The MRI had revealed absolutely nothing out of the ordinary, but when the surgeon cut in, he determined that he needed to remove a major portion of William's disk.

But the pain remained.

What do you do when the answer is no? Three surgeries in, and God was not providing William with any relief from the pain that was keeping him from doing his job as a physician, a provider for his family, a father.

A lumbar puncture, shooting contrast fluid up the spine— maybe this would help determine what was wrong? And yet, a procedure that was supposed to be painless produced the most searing pain William had ever experienced in his life. Instead of filling the middle of the spine, the injected fluid caused a condition called arachnoiditis, in which all of the spider-like membranes that surround and protect the nerves of the central nervous system were filled with the errant fluid. The shooting pain snaked everywhere: down through his legs, his groin, his crotch, producing burning heat and freezing cold. His back was so ultrasensitive that he couldn't even endure clothing touching his skin.

Nights became stretches of psychotic dreams; days were spent passed out on the couch with kids running around, and an alarmed wife realizing that her husband was not even able to be home alone and entrusted with their care. It was the darkest period of William's life.

Everything was crashing. Everything. Amid the physical pain that William was enduring, there was the fear of sinking into debt, job loss, the stigma he felt being on disability and pain medications, all of which were threatening to undo him. The surgeon who had walked alongside him up to this point announced that he wouldn't do William's planned fusion surgery. What options were left?

As concerned mothers tend to do, William's mom persisted, once again suggesting the healing ministry at a church called Bethel. This time, William was listening. As a physician who knew God, William would regularly pray over patients, asking God to heal with all power and authority. Easy to say and do, but not easy to apply to his own circumstances.

"I could hear God saying to me, 'You want to heal and help others, but why don't you trust me to heal you?' I could give, but I couldn't receive. I've wanted my whole life to receive, but if I was on the receiving end, then I wasn't in control. My identity was so wrapped up in my self-sufficiency, I didn't have a clue of my identity in Christ."

A group of men surrounded William, and together they made the trek to Bethel, in pursuit of God and the healing he might provide there. What William didn't know was that the night before, while he was sleeping the most peaceful sleep he had experienced in years, his wife Kari had been up all night praying for William, pleading with God to heal him and make him whole. The next morning, William could already feel the beginning of the healing process: "The whole experience at Bethel, beginning with the support and prayer of the guys who went with me, and then the unhindered worship and the freedom to pray—all of it made me realize how limited I'd made God in my control of him.

"I stood on the platform with the group that was praying for us, and as they asked me what led up to my back issues, I told them that I had never had an accident or singular event that caused the problems I was having. One woman broke from the conversation and asked, 'Is there anything in your life that you've always wanted but never had? Something that hasn't been fulfilled?'"

Will froze. He had always longed for a whole relationship with his dad, a man who had raised him at arm's length and with no boundaries, a man who himself didn't understand the depth of God's exhaustive love for him. By the power of the Holy Spirit, the woman at Bethel knew that William's pain wasn't merely physical; there was a spiritual component that might have an impact on his recovery.

The Holy Spirit brought healing to William that day, but the remedy would not alleviate his physical pain. When William returned home, he sought to restore the relationship with his dad— something that both men knew could take place only through the deliverance of a holy God. The generational hedges that had been erected and plagued their contact and communication for decades were being supernaturally torn down and replaced with the pure and beautiful love of God the Father.

I want to tell you that William's back injury and pain are resolved. He would like to tell you that too, but the truth is that William's pain has returned, and he has exhausted every avenue to manage it, from surgeries to physical therapy, from counseling to a lumbar nerve ablation, and to the implantation of a nerve stimulator in the summer of 2012. The truth is, life is difficult and doesn't always get tied up so neatly. Many, many times we cannot know relief, healing, or an answer to our most difficult trials. William might always live with pain that keeps him from practicing medicine in an emergency room; Mighty Joe will always have six holes in his brain.

But we're not left to wallow there. William has hope because he knows that his grand story has yet to be completed. Although he's deep in the fall of his career and health, God has a plan to redeem and restore him, beginning with a return to the complete truth of the gospel and the discovery of his true identity in what Christ has done for him. All this is woven into the pain and the radical disruption of what he thought would be the direction of his life.

God has not abandoned William. He has not abandoned Mighty Joe. He has promised us a plan that gives us a hope and a future, and he will see that plan to fruition, either here or in eternity, where our identity with the One who loves us beyond measure will be complete. Remember? God is in the business of rebuilding and restoring broken lives. However we lose our way, we are never so lost that God cannot find us and restore us to himself.

And it is God who establishes us with you in Christ, and has anointed us, and who has also put his seal on us and given us his Spirit in our hearts as a guarantee. (2 Corinthians 1:21–22)

Are you tired of
"do more, try harder" religion?

Key Life has only one message, to communicate the radical grace of God to sinners and sufferers. Because of what Jesus has done, God's not mad at you.

KEY LIFE
God's not mad at you

On radio, in print, on CDs and online, we're proclaiming the scandalous reality of Jesus' good news of radical grace…leading to radical freedom, infectious joy and surprising faithfulness to Christ.

For all things grace, visit us at **KeyLife.org**